M000306858

"Fr. Dwight Longenecker never c[...] culture of death with lucidity, shining the light of Christ on its darkness. Who else could connect sin with Sinatra, Disneyworld with Aldous Huxley, prophecy with Puddleglum, and barbarism with Barbie dolls? In a world lulled to sleep by the wicked witch of the decadent West, Fr. Longenecker wakens us with the fire of faith, vivid writing, and a fertile imagination."

—**Joseph Pearce**
Biographer and editor of the *St. Austin Review*

"Fr. Longenecker has long been one of the clearest contemporary commentators on our current crisis. In this incisive and readable volume, he not only takes us through the new forms that the world, the flesh, and the devil have assumed in our times. Even more importantly, he provides strong, practical suggestions for fighting and winning the perennial battle with evil."

—**Robert Royal, Ph.D.**
President, Faith & Reason Institute

"By combining the incisive analytical power of worldview apologetics with a rich imaginative vision that moves smoothly between high culture and pop culture, Fr. Dwight accurately identifies the lies that have led our modern world astray and offers real solutions for getting us back on track. In between, he offers a dramatic dialogue with the devil that fleshes out the nature of the crisis and the immensity of the deception in an entertaining and memorable way."

—**Louis Markos**
Professor in English and scholar in residence at Houston Baptist University; author of *Atheism on Trial: Refuting the Modern Arguments against God*

"We live in a difficult age marked by constant flux and in which traditional ways of thinking are under seemingly constant attack. To be a faithful Christian at such a moment is not easy, and there is no simple spiritual vaccine or silver bullet that can solve our problems. Nor does Fr. Longenecker offer such. Instead, he offers a thorough and multifaceted diagnosis of our present condition and a solution—or rather, a complex of solutions, rooted in a recovery and application of Christian truths. Practically grounded in repentance and metaphysically grounded in an understanding of ourselves as given identity by, and answerable to, God, the proposals of this accessible yet profound book will fortify pastors and laypeople alike as they seek to be salt and light in this world."

—**Carl R. Trueman**
Grove City College and author of *The Rise and Triumph*
of the Modern Self: Cultural Amnesia, Expressive
Individualism, and the Road to Sexual Revolution

"The English writer Samuel Johnson once struck his foot against a large stone, and exclaimed, 'I refute it thus'—referring to the seemingly irrefutable theory of Berkeley: that matter does not exist. Can modern materialism be refuted? 'Tithe your income,' Fr. Longenecker tells us, and exclaim while you do, 'I refute it thus!' Can utilitarianism be refuted? 'Spend a summer as a missionary,' he proposes, saying to yourself, 'I refute it thus!' And so with the other fourteen beguiling isms that make up the monstrous many-headed Hydra—our culture—which deceives and haunts us all."

—**Michael Pakaluk**
Philosopher and author of *The Memoirs of St. Peter*
and *Mary's Voice in the Gospel according to John*

"Fr. Longenecker has given us a highly readable analysis of the many false ideologies — isms—that beset us and keen guidance on how to defeat them. But he wears his learning lightly. This is no turgid tome. On the contrary, never has intellectual history been more entertaining! You should read this for both enlightenment and encouragement."

—Jay W. Richards
**Research assistant professor, Busch School of Business,
The Catholic University of America**

"This is an excellent diagnosis of the ills of modern culture. Its genius lies in linking those ills to creatively subversive responses that reinforce Christian culture at the local level."

—Joseph T. Stuart, Ph.D.
**Associate professor of history and fellow in
Catholic studies, University of Mary, and author of
*Rethinking the Enlightenment: Faith in the Age of Reason***

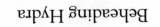

Beheading Hydra

Also by Dwight Longenecker:

Immortal Combat

An Answer, Not an Argument

Our Lady? A Catholic/Evangelical Debate

St. Benedict and St. Thérèse: The Little Rule and The Little Way

Listen My Son: St. Benedict for Fathers

The Gargoyle Code

Slubgrip Instructs

Catholicism Pure and Simple

More Christianity

The Mystery of the Magi

Praying the Rosary for Inner Healing

Praying the Rosary for Spiritual Warfare

A Sudden Certainty

The Quest for the Creed

The Romance of Religion

Letters on Liturgy

Available at Amazon and at
dwightlongenecker.com

Fr. Dwight Longenecker

Beheading Hydra

A Radical Plan for Christians
in an Atheistic Age

SOPHIA INSTITUTE PRESS
Manchester, New Hampshire

Copyright © 2021 by Fr. Dwight Longenecker

Printed in the United States of America. All rights reserved.

Cover design by David Ferris Design (www.davidferrisdesign.com).

Cover image: Engraving of the second labor of Heracles
(MW424E) © The Picture Art Collection / Alamy.

Unless otherwise noted, Scripture texts in this work are taken from the
New American Bible, revised edition © 2010, 1991, 1986, 1970 Confraternity
of Christian Doctrine, Washington, D.C. and are used by permission of the
copyright owner. All Rights Reserved. No part of the *New American Bible* may
be reproduced in any form without permission in writing from the copyright
owner.

No part of this book may be reproduced, stored in a retrieval system, or trans-
mitted in any form, or by any means, electronic, mechanical, photocopying,
or otherwise, without the prior written permission of the publisher, except by
a reviewer, who may quote brief passages in a review.

Sophia Institute Press
Box 5284, Manchester, NH 03108
1-800-888-9344

www.SophiaInstitute.com

Sophia Institute Press® is a registered trademark of Sophia Institute.

paperback ISBN 978-1-64413-490-0

ebook ISBN 978-1-64413-491-7

Library of Congress Control Number: 2021938642

First printing

To Jim Craft

How good and how pleasant it is,
when brothers dwell together as one!

—Psalm 133:1

Contents

Foreword

We live in troubled times. In 2020, America's politics and economy were sent on a roller-coaster ride by a pandemic, riots, and an election that was marked by extraordinary vitriol, even by American standards.

But there is trouble, and there is *trouble*. The travails of America, and the West in general, go far beyond the challenges associated with the world's struggle against an invisible enemy in what many people would describe as the most depressing year of their lives. That is one of the core messages of Fr. Dwight Longenecker's reflections on the many-headed beast that is relentlessly corroding the foundations of Western civilization. It's very easy to get caught up in the immediate difficulties confronting us while forgetting the deeper, often centuries-old forces that are at work in the world and at war with the true, the good, and the beautiful.

The problem, Fr. Longenecker states, is that these forces are part of the air we breathe. It is simply assumed, even by many small-o orthodox Christians and Jews, that reason and faith have nothing to do with each other, that science disproves the claims of religion, that happiness is whatever brings pleasure to the greatest number of people, that what is new is always good, and that everyone is going to Heaven, not matter how much evil they have done and how unrepentant they may be for their actions.

It's also painfully obvious that many of those who presumably would be willing, if not eager, to illustrate the fallacies underlying these positions—Catholic and Orthodox priests, Evangelical pastors, Jewish rabbis, assorted theologians—are often afraid to do so. In some instances, it is because they are afraid of upsetting people. In other instances, they have actually bought into these fallacies themselves.

As readers of *Beheading Hydra* will soon discover, Fr. Dwight Longenecker is not one of those people. He is more than willing to call out the errors of our time—scientism, materialism, utilitarianism, and sentimental humanitarianism, to name just a few—and to explain how they came to be and how they have worked their way into our everyday lives. In doing so, he uses everyday language to unpack the core problems with these ideas and the manner in which they shape the very words we speak. You know that people have, perhaps subconsciously, bought into these ways of thought when they begin arguments by saying, "I just feel that ..." rather than, "I think that is the case, and here is the evidence that I believe provides proof of the truth of my position."

Theologians and philosophers from different Christian confessions have been addressing many of these problems for at least five centuries. In truth, the modernist errors go back even further. Sophism and materialism were alive and well in Plato and Aristotle's time. From that standpoint, there are no new heresies in the world. There are also well-worked-out responses to these errors to be found in books written by figures such as Augustine of Hippo in the twilight of the Roman Empire, Thomas Aquinas in the medieval period, and Joseph Ratzinger in the late twentieth century.

In most cases, however, engaging in these discussions requires a great deal of theological, philosophical, and historical knowledge and preparation. And therein lies the great strength of this book. Longenecker explains in simple yet vivid terms what we confront, using examples to which all of us can immediately relate, to show how, for instance, sentimentalism destroys our capacity to engage in reasoned debate, or why materialism doesn't meet the demand of reason, including scientific and empirical reason. This is the type of formation in ideas that those who are bewildered by the apparent chaos around them need to receive.

Part of that formation involves showing how the various errors that surround us are all related to, and feed upon, each other. Materialism and scientism reinforce each other. So, too, do utilitarianism, moral relativism, and the idea that all religions are basically the same (indifferentism) and therefore equally irrelevant. If you embrace materialism, either as a philosophical position or as a lifestyle, it's hardly surprising that you start to think that reason cannot know any truth beyond that which is empirical, measurable, and quantifiable. And if that is your conception of reason, you can't help but start to see the world in materialist terms.

All this points to the need for a radical intervention, one that will break the cycle in which error supports error—a cycle that results in people finding themselves locked in a hall of blurry mirrors that give a distorted vision of reality. Longenecker's recommended form of intervention is what he calls "creative subversion." By this, he doesn't mean a type of furious confrontation, or playing clever accommodationist games that turn out (as we should have learned from the late 1960s onward) to produce colossal pastoral and intellectual failures such as the Catholic and Lutheran churches in Germany, as even many progressive and liberal Christians will today concede. Instead, "creative sub-version" means, to paraphrase Longenecker, sidestepping the subtle lies, rolling up one's sleeves, and doing whatever we can wherever we are, with whatever we have.

This, Longenecker says, is the path of radical discipleship. It eschews dialogue for the sake of dialogue and pretending that those preaching errors are always people of goodwill. Instead, Longenecker describes a life of disciplined prayer, a rigorous self-examination to discern whether practical materialism or practical atheism has made inroads into our lives, treating the sacraments as what they really are—rather than just rites of passage—and believing that God is not simply involved in history but is also involved and interested in our own histories. These and other forms of personal conversion will, Longenecker believes, provide space for God to work through our lives and gradually corrode the errors in which so much of the modern world has buried its head.

Therein lies the radicalness of the Christian message, as lived by the first Christians. Fr. Longenecker demonstrates that, more than ever, the world needs to hear that message and the Church needs to live it. In this book, he shows us how.

—Samuel Gregg
Research Director
Acton Institute

Acknowledgments

Beheading Hydra emerged from the first half of a completely different book. Thanks go to Charlie McKinney and the team at Sophia Institute Press for being flexible with this process and seeing how two books could come out of an original idea.

Thanks to the Norbertine Sisters at Bethlehem Priory in the mountains of central California for inviting me to lead their retreat and for offering monastic solitude for me to write and to test the opening chapters on them.

Kevin O'Brien, Roger Thomas, Jim Craft, Sid Tate, Vincent Weaver, and Sr. Mary Norbert read the manuscript and offered good feedback. I also thank my friends Gilbert, Jack, Tom, Ben, and Rose for their prayers and protection.

Finally, thanks to Alison, who is always supportive even if some books "have too many words."

Greenville, South Carolina
January 25, 2021
Feast of the Conversion of St. Paul

Part 1

The Many-Headed Hydra

Do not love the world or the things of the world. If anyone loves the world, the love of the Father is not in him. For all that is in the world, sensual lust, enticement for the eyes, and a pretentious life, is not from the Father but is from the world. Yet the world and its enticement are passing away. But whoever does the will of God remains forever.

Children, it is the last hour; and just as you heard that the antichrist was coming, so now many antichrists have appeared. Thus we know this is the last hour.

—1 John 2:15–19

Introduction to the Problem

The Many-Headed Hydra

A few years ago, when we were on a family vacation at Myrtle Beach, I dared the kids to go through one of those walk-through spook houses with me. It was terrifying fun. We had to feel our way through dark corridors where most any sort of horror could be lurking.

Suddenly the door of a closet would swing open, and a zombie would moan and reach for us; or as we turned a corner, a creep dressed as a chain-saw killer would leap out and chase us down the corridor where who knew what other ghastly, ghostly terror might assault us. It was fun because we knew the various ghouls couldn't harm us and that, five minutes later, we'd be out on the boardwalk again, laughing at our lily-livered selves.

The fear in the house of horrors was bad enough, but the real terror was not knowing what was coming next. Was a mad-woman with wild hair and brandishing a knife lurking behind the curtain, or was the next fright some unimaginable demon beast? Or was it a werewolf, Medusa and her sisters, a chupacabra, or the three-headed hound of Hell? Who knew?

Not wishing to exaggerate too much, but writing at the end of 2020, I cannot help but note that this year, while not exactly the house of horrors, has plunged many people into a spook house of stress and the extremes of bewilderment, uncertainty, suspicion, and fear.

A distressing pandemic followed by economic hardship, social unrest, and a contentious general election in the United States swept many up in a whirlwind of insecurity. At the same time, Catholics continued to be thrown into their own swirl of uncertainty by doctrinal confusion, financial corruption, sexual immorality, political sellouts at the highest level of the Church, and a pope who seemed to contribute to the mess.

Uncertain times, of course, are nothing new. In every age, our human family has been caught up in storms of every kind. "Three hundred years before the resurrection ... Thucydides wrote describing the decline of the world's culture around him ... and three hundred years after the resurrection St. Basil the Great wrote describing the collapse of Roman imperial civilization."[1] History shows that there have always been wars and rumors of wars, natural disasters, plagues, famines, and distress. If you read a history of the church, you will soon realize that corrupt cardinals, hypocritical prelates, and incompetent popes are also nothing new.

The troubles of 2020 have hit hard because many of us in America had gotten used to an affluent, comfortable, trouble-free life. As writer John Horvat has noted, we had enjoyed a cruise-ship culture in which everyone was living the good life and sailing along merrily with an exuberant economy, plenty of food, and constant entertainment.[2] But this is not real. We

---

[1] Fr George Rutler, *A Crisis in Culture* (Manchester, NH: Sophia Institute Press, 2020), 75.

[2] John Horvat, "Is This the End of Our 'Cruise-Ship Economy'?," *Imaginative Conservative*, October 19, 2020, https://theimaginativeconservative.org/2020/10/this-end-our-cruise-ship-economy-john-horvat.html

should remember the great struggles and turmoil suffered by our parents, grandparents, and ancestors.

One hundred years ago, the world was staggering forth from the horrors of the First World War, bloody revolutions, and a flu pandemic. The troubles seemed overwhelming and the future ominous. In 1920, the Irish poet William Butler Yeats was caught up in the Irish War of Independence. His pregnant wife nearly died in the flu pandemic, and all around him, Europe was reeling from the effects of war and the upheavals of revolution.

Yeats's poem "The Second Coming" perfectly expresses the atmosphere of fear and foreboding. Things are bad, but what worse horrors lurk around the corner and down the next corridor?

> Turning and turning in the widening gyre
> The falcon cannot hear the falconer;
> Things fall apart; the centre cannot hold;
> Mere anarchy is loosed upon the world,
> The blood-dimmed tide is loosed, and everywhere
> The ceremony of innocence is drowned;
> The best lack all conviction, while the worst
> Are full of passionate intensity.
> Surely some revelation is at hand;
> Surely the Second Coming is at hand.
> The Second Coming! Hardly are those words out
> When a vast image out of Spiritus Mundi
> Troubles my sight: somewhere in sands of the desert
> A shape with lion body and the head of a man,
> A gaze blank and pitiless as the sun,
> Is moving its slow thighs, while all about it
> Reel shadows of the indignant desert birds.

Beheading Hydra

The darkness drops again; but now I know
That twenty centuries of stony sleep
Were vexed to nightmare by a rocking cradle,
And what rough beast, its hour come round at last,
Slouches towards Bethlehem to be born?[3]

What's going on in our world? Are things heading toward a terrible climax, or is it simply that we are in the middle of turmoil and unrest, as the human race has been in every age?

Both are true. Every age has seen change, revolution, and uncertainty, but we are also at a turning point. In his book *Bad Religion: How We Became a Nation of Heretics*, Ross Douthat analyzes the reasons for the present religious crisis in the United States. Coming out of the Second World War, America enjoyed a renaissance of religion. Churches were full, families were growing, Christian morality was taken for granted, and religious leaders such as Billy Graham and Fulton Sheen were riding high. Then everything crashed. Douthat identifies five causes for the sudden nosedive.

The first was political division. Christians fell into right- or left-wing tribes, depending on their views on various social issues, such as the Vietnam War and abortion. Second was the invention of the birth control pill and the subsequent sexual revolution. Third was an increasingly mobile population and global perspective. This caused many people to regard their own religion as just another faith among many. Fourth was the growing affluence in America. Put simply, people who have everything don't think they need God. Finally, as Americans became more educated,

---

[3] Charles Coffin, ed., *The Major Poets English and American* (New York: Harcourt Brace and World, 1969), 467.

they increasingly regarded Christianity as ignorant, low-class, and not worthy of their attention.[4]

As a result, we are experiencing a colossal collapse of organized Christianity. Douthat quotes the sobering statistics: In 1966, the Catholic Church boasted 60,000 priests, 12,000 religious brothers, and 180,000 religious sisters. By 1969, 2 percent of priests had abandoned their vocation; by 1980, seminary enrollment fell by two-thirds, and religious sisters left in droves.[5] The falloff rate in the mainstream Protestant denominations during the sixties, seventies, and eighties was even more acute. And today? According to a 2018 report by the U.S. Conference of Catholic Bishops, there are about 37,000 priests, 4,000 brothers, and just 45,000 sisters.

Clearly, the great Christian nation of America has stumbled. The crisis of faith is combined with a philosophical implosion and a cultural and moral maelstrom all at the same time. Technological innovation, increasing affluence, social mobility, and shifts in our values have brought about a crisis in our culture. The philosophical foundations rumbled like an underwater earthquake far off the coast, but now the tsunami caused by the earthquake is crashing in, threatening to sweep over everything.

The anxiety at the beginning of the 2020s is not simply the result of a pandemic and a contentious political climate. These surface problems are only the catalyst for a stress storm that has much deeper causes. This perfect storm is the culmination of five hundred years of devious philosophies, half-truths, godless ideologies, false religions, and rebellion against God, His Church, and His timeless truths.

---

[4]   Ross Douthat, *Bad Religion: How We Became a Nation of Heretics* (New York: Doubleday, 2012), 65–82.

[5]   Ibid., 60.

These deceptions are the foundation of the modern world. Living in the high-tech twenty-first century is like dancing on quicksand. Nothing seems certain. Everything shifts. The center cannot hold.

The Modern Mind

What we believe affects how we behave, and how we behave affects what we believe. Ideas matter because we live out our lives according to our beliefs. It follows that false philosophies and distorted ideologies will lead to uncertainty, confusion, and fear. Lies produce more lies. Deception is layered with further deception. The people of the lie live, breathe, and promulgate lies. They mentally and spiritually copulate to populate the world with more and more lies.

The chapters that follow outline the contours of the modern mindset. I don't pretend that this is an exhaustive treatment. I am not a philosopher by any stretch. This is not a scholarly treatise or a complete explanation. For a genuine intellectual analysis, read Carl Trueman's book *The Rise and Triumph of the Modern Self*. But this book is a sketch rather than a portrait, a prophetic polemic rather than a detached and intellectual analysis. It's written as a battle plan, not a doctoral thesis.

Every good battle plan involves a thorough knowledge of the enemy. Satan is a liar and the Father of Lies, and to counter his lies, we need to understand them. He is the prince of this world, so we should expect to find his lies embedded in the philosophies of this world.

The belief system of modern man is difficult to define because it is not specified and systematic. It is a worldview without a label and a religion without a creed. Instead, it is a compendium of lies, a catalogue of deceptions, a septic tank of subterfuge. The lies are never explicit in our society. They lurk beneath the surface as a set of assumptions; at times, they slither and slide on the surface, but then they disappear below again, only to reappear in a different form.

These lies are not an aspect of the culture. They *are* the culture. They are the wallpaper. They are the air we breathe. The lies are woven in and through the media, advertising, film, literature, and the educational establishment. They are not questioned because they lurk beneath our consciousness. The web of lies is "simply the way things are." These dark deceptions are the foundation of the culture, and who stops to dig down and examine the foundations of the house in which they live?

Furthermore, this network of lies has infiltrated the Christian church. They have not only infected the theology, but our Christian leaders themselves have baptized the lies, thereby promoting as Christianity a religion that is, in fact, the religion of the Antichrist.

To complicate things further, this set of assumptions is not fixed. It is constantly shifting and morphing. The language is constantly changing. The form in which the lies are expressed is forever swirling and deceiving like smoke and mirrors. Just as you are getting a grip on one expression, the terminology changes. This lie fades away but returns in a subtler and more alluring form. That lie disappears, but another, more seductive and noxious one takes its place.

This shifty nature of the modernist mindset explains why so many people in our age are confused, bewildered, and afraid. They are lost in the desert; they teeter on the edge of a precipice where there is no foothold. The constantly morphing nature of the lies should not surprise us because they are the product of the great serpent himself, the monstrous chameleon, the Father of Lies.

Clarity in this smoke-and-mirrors world, however, can be achieved in one simple step. It requires courage. It requires a bold, bracing splash in the face with the icy water of truth. Pope John Paul II said there were two materialistic, atheistic world systems: communism and unrestrained capitalism. Americans don't like to hear this, but it is true. The problem with the American form of atheism is that it is woven through the system in such subtle ways that, in our confusion, we cannot see it for what it is.

To understand the real heart of darkness, we need some straight talk. We must choose to recognize the lies for what they are: different masks of atheism — and atheism is itself a costume of the Antichrist, who seethes with pure hatred of God and his Truth.

Rip off the masks of atheism and strip bare the Antichrist. Decide to see through the elaborate costumes. They are not simply "modernism" or "post-modernism." We do not simply live in a "post-Christian society." We live in a society that is deeply atheistic and therefore anti-Christian, and if anti-Christian, then increasingly antagonistic toward Christians themselves.

Do not be deceived any longer, and do not put your head in the sand. Now is the time to wake out of sleep. "Now many antichrists have appeared" (1 John 2:18). Do not be naïve and tell yourself that it is not really so bad. Do not be afraid that you might be thought to be a paranoid conspiracy theorist. It is not a conspiracy when the enemies speak openly about their plans. We are at that stage now. The enemies are clear about their ambitions. The dragon, who was so long hidden in his underground lair is stirring. He is ready to deceive openly and ready to breathe fire on his foes.

The Hydra

Another powerful serpentine image that illustrates the battle at hand is the Hydra — the mythical water serpent that lurked in the swamps of Lake Lerna—one of the entrances to the underworld. In the ancient myth, the Hydra's blood and venom were so poisonous that even their stench was deadly.

Instead of one head, the terrible monster of the underworld had many—all of them writhing and twisting, fanged and venomous. When one head was cut off, two more grew back in its place. Socrates used the Hydra as an illustration of the deceitful person who, when his argument is proved to be a lie, immediately comes up with two more arguments.

The Hydra is a perfect illustration of the beast that dominates the modern world. The lies that populate the modernist mind are like the many heads of the Hydra. Cut one off with the weapons of truth, beauty, and goodness, and two more-venomous heads grow in its place.

In the following chapters, we will examine sixteen heads of the modernist Hydra. These *isms* are the core assumptions of the modern world, but they are not the only ones. From each fanged head, many others sprout and grow to writhe and sway like a cobra before they strike.

Like the heads of the Hydra, the sixteen isms seem to have lives of their own, but in fact they interweave with each other, spawn in their spit, and replicate. Behead any of them, and it returns in slightly different form because they are all connected to the immortal body of their dragon host.

The third part of the first half of the book is written as a dramatic dialogue between a representative of Satan and a questioner. That chapter summarizes the sixteen isms and reveals the true result and end point of the devious ideologies and philosophies.

When Christ the Lord went into the wilderness to do battle with Satan, He was offered three temptations: the kingdoms of the world, the satisfaction of His flesh, and the worship of the devil. These three categories of the world, the flesh, and the devil provide a way to categorize the lies of the modern swamp.

Unlike the Hydra, who was truly monstrous in appearance, however, the Hydra heads we will consider do not appear terrible at first. Satan smiles before he snarls. Indeed, like all of Satan's lies, they are seductive, alluring, and, if you have no defense, irresistible. If you are unaware of them, their power over you is all the greater.

Only with clear analysis can we see past their pleasant appearance to glimpse the terrible monster behind the mask and realize that the fangs of the Hydra are venomous indeed; and if we develop the nose for it, we'll realize that even one whiff of their stench is enough to kill.

Whereas the first half of the book is a grim walk through the horror house of our modern culture, the second half of the book presents the joyful, powerful, and practical actions that can be taken to behead the Hydra. The second part of the book has its own introduction, so now, take courage, turn the page, and meet the Hydra.

The World

In the wilderness, Satan tempted the Lord Jesus Christ by offering him all the kingdoms of the world. Therefore the first eight isms we will examine concern the philosophies that lie behind the politics and power structures of this world.

1

The Holy Prophet Puddleglum

Materialism and Atheism

Puddleglum is a Marshwiggle. Those who have read *The Silver Chair* will remember C. S. Lewis's description of this resident of Narnia. On first sighting, the two children, Jill Pole and Eustace Scrubb, observe the strange creature: its narrow face, sunken cheeks, tight lips, and pointy nose. The Marshwiggle is very serious, in the way that ridiculous people tend to be. "Good morning, guests," says Puddleglum. "Though when I say *good*, I don't mean it won't probably turn to rain or it might be snow, or fog, or thunder. You didn't get any sleep I dare say."[6]

Now, Puddleglum is well named because he lives in a puddle and he is glum. As we get to know him, we learn that his pessimism hides a shrewd intelligence. He may be glum, but he's not gullible. He becomes the guide for the children in their adventure to find Prince Rilian, who has been kidnapped by the queen of the underworld—she of the Green Kirtle, whom we will nickname the Green Queen.

Eventually their quest leads them into the caverns where the Green Queen has put Prince Rilian under a spell and enslaved

[6]   C. S. Lewis, *The Silver Chair* (New York: Collier Books, 1971), 58.

15

him. When Puddleglum and the children free him and try to escape, the Green Queen puts all of them under an enchantment. Using deceptive logic, a seductive siren song, and intoxicating smoke, she convinces them that there is no beautiful land of Narnia. The blue sky, the sun, the moon, the stars, and the land aboveground are all figments of their imagination, and they are fools to believe that such a place as Narnia exists.

Her kingdom of Underland is all that is. She tries to convince the others that Narnia — the beautiful country where all is noble and innocent — is no more than a fond wish, a vain dream, and a silly fantasy.

What You See Is What You Get

What the Green Queen was selling was old-fashioned material-ism. Now, when I say "materialism," I don't mean going to the mall to shop until you drop. I don't mean simply grabbing at more and more possessions in the belief that they will make you happy. Greed is merely one of the symptoms of materialism.

Materialism itself is the main head of the Hydra. Put simply, it is the proposal that this physical world is all there is. What you see is what you get. It is "the conviction that everything, including reason, is a product of the material world, that at the root of everything is not a Creator ... that freely chooses to bring the material world into being and sustain it. There is just material."[7]

Like all of the venomous Hydra heads, materialism is rarely proclaimed explicitly. Few people argue openly for materialism. They don't need to. The entire culture has fallen under the spell

---

[7] Samuel Gregg, *Reason, Faith, and the Struggle for Western Civilization* (Washington, DC: Regnery Gateway, 2019), 137.

of the Green Queen. Instead of an open statement of materialism, the materialist point of view is expressed in the form of mockery.

Should the materialist discover that you are a religious believer, he may well quiz you: "Do you pray? What about demons and angels? Really? Do you also believe in your lucky stars? Santa Claus with his eight tiny reindeer? Elves and dwarves and ogres and trolls and tree spirits and wee leprechauns? The tooth fairy? Tinkerbell? I know: if you believe in fairies, clap your hands!"

Should you confess belief in the afterlife, the matter-of-fact materialist will scoff at the idea of Heaven and Hell. "Heaven, Hell, and Purgatory? That's just the wishful thinking of folks who are afraid to die. They invent fanciful destinations where they think they'll live happily ever after. But that is all make-believe."

Humming that tune by John Lennon, the materialist says, "Imagine there's no Heaven.... Imagine there's no Hell." Then he delivers his brutal denial. "There is no life after death. When you take your last breath, it's a flat line. Nada. Zilch. The lights go out. The curtain drops. That's it. The end."

Life after Death

Being embarrassed to admit your belief in Heaven, Hell, angels, and demons, you might retort to the materialist, "But surely you believe in life after death, don't you? What about your soul? We all must end up somewhere!"

To which he will reply, "But what evidence is there for any kind of consciousness surviving physical death; and for that matter, what exactly is your soul?"

"There are plenty of near-death experiences," you reply. "People die and see Heaven or Hell, and then they come back to tell the story."

"Then they didn't really die, did they?" says the materialist with a condescending smile. Besides, we now know that these experiences are caused by a release of enzymes in the brain — the same ones that produce hallucinations. It's simply a brain burp — a little chemical in the brain hiccup as the body gives up the ghost."

"You just said 'gives up the ghost'! So you do believe in the soul after all!"

"It was simply a turn of phrase. A metaphor. No more."

Do you see how difficult it is to cut off a head of the Hydra?

A Universal Majority

Putting aside the specifics of Heaven, Hell, angels, demons, leprechauns, and the tooth fairy, the basic bottom line is whether one believes in an invisible realm of reality or not. "All questions come down at last to the assertion or denial of a reality independent of the mind which we can know by means of the mind with certainty."[8]

What do I mean by an independent or invisible realm of reality? I mean a dimension of existence that is beyond our normal sense perception. We call it "supernatural," meaning "above or greater than nature." Unfortunately, that definition is somewhat misleading because when people hear "above nature," they conclude that the supernatural realm is up in the sky. It would be more accurate to say that this realm is *beyond* nature, but even this is not quite right because the supernatural is not only beyond the natural realm. It also infuses and flows through the natural realm like electricity through the power grid.

8   John Senior, *The Restoration of Catholic Culture* (Norfolk, VA: IHS Press, 2008), 107.

Let me simplify: everything physical will, given enough time, rot, rust, die, decay, and disappear. The invisible realm of reality is not physical; therefore, it is not bound by time or the decay for which material things are destined. This supernatural realm, because it is eternal, is superior to the material realm of dust, dirt, death, and decay. That is not to say that the physical realm is unimportant or bad, however, because it is through the physical, material realm that we experience the invisible, eternal realm.

What has always tickled me is the arrogant assumption of the materialists, that their disbelief in the invisible realm is somehow not only obvious, but that it is the majority opinion of all ordinary, practically minded people who "don't bother with all that superstitious, fanciful nonsense."

In fact, the opposite is true. The vast majority of the human race in all places and cultures down through the ages have been supernaturalists. Most people throughout history have believed in God, and most people today do as well. They believe in life after death, spirit beings, and the possibility of interaction between the visible world and the invisible.

Religion is so basic and distinctive to our humanity that we might as well be called *homo orans* (praying man) rather than *homo sapiens* (thinking man). From the burial cairns of Neanderthals to an astronaut reading the Bible on his way to the moon, mankind is innately religious, and religion presupposes a fundamental belief in the invisible, eternal realm.

Even those who don't go to church and who will not commit to believing in angels and demons or Heaven and Hell still hold to some sort of vague belief in the spiritual realm. They hope to see their departed loved ones again. They dabble in horoscopes and palmistry, give meditation a try, and watch documentaries about the Day of the Dead. They nod their head when Obi-Wan says "May the Force be with you," and even the doubters get chills when they hear stories of exorcisms, hauntings, and miracles.

It is the materialists who are in the minority, and in their intellectual arrogance, they look down on the vast majority of good, ordinary human beings who believe there is more in Heaven and earth than their materialist philosophy has dreamed of.

Under a Spell

The real problem with most materialists is not that they deny the existence of the invisible realm but that they are cowardly and lazy. They have not had the guts or the gumption to follow their disbelief to the end point.

It is all well and good to pooh-pooh the tooth fairy and snigger at those who believe in guardian angels, hellfire, brimstone, and the sweet by-and-by. It's easy enough to sneer at the rubes who believe in Heaven and Hell, but what is the end point of materialism? What is the ultimate position of one who disbelieves in the invisible realm?

The end point of materialism must be atheism, and this is the second head of the Hydra. It is obvious, isn't it? If one does not believe in the invisible realm, dismisses the existence of life after death, Heaven, Hell, and all the rest, then it must follow that one cannot believe in God either, because God, by very definition, is the ultimate, invisible reality.

Most materialists, however, would not claim to be atheists. That might upset their mothers-in-law or their nice suburban neighbors. Most American materialists are default atheists. They don't so much disbelieve in God as they never give God a thought at all. They go about their daily lives eating, working, playing, sleeping—never considering what's to come and never giving the eternal realm a second thought.

The typical American is completely under the enchantment of the Green Queen. Now that is *real* atheism, and that is the true triumph of materialism—that most atheists are blind to the fact that they are atheists.

The thinkers of the seventeenth and eighteenth centuries understood where it was all headed. For eons, mankind had believed in the reality of the invisible realm. It was not questioned. Then, in the fourteenth century, a little English heresy called nominalism put its toe in the door.[9] The nominalists said the so-called realities of the invisible realm were no more than the names we give them.

This pulled the rug out from beneath the Catholic sacramental system, so when the Protestants finally abandoned that beautiful, God-given, integrated system that links earth and Heaven—the system that said that invisible realities were communicated through the physical realm—there was a great divorce not only in the Church but also in society and in every Christian soul between the head, the heart, and the body.

There was no longer a connection between the two realms, and once that link was broken, it was not long before everyone was investing heavily in the visible realm and gradually disbelieving in the invisible realm. While the study of science burgeoned, philosophy and theology became more abstract and cut off from the physical world, so God became more distant. Instead of an intimate, immanent God, He was pushed out to a cloudy hideaway.

---

9   Learn more about nominalism and realism in Maurice De Wulf, "Nominalism, Realism, Conceptualism," *Catholic Encyclopedia*, vol. 11 (New York: Robert Appleton, 1911), New Advent, https://www.newadvent.org/cathen/11090c.htm.

Beheading Hydra

By the seventeenth and eighteenth centuries, thinkers were trying to tiptoe around the obvious conclusion, which was atheism. Diderot, Voltaire, Benjamin Franklin, and the rest of the "enlightened ones" devised another intellectual sleight of hand called Deism. According to the Deists, God jump-started the whole physical world and then retired. They professed belief in God but suggested that He never got involved in this world.

But what sort of God is that? I'd rather have Zeus or Ganesh the elephant god than the God of the Deists. At least they *do* something.

Is there really any difference between a Deist and an atheist except a set of manners and the wish to assume a safe position that does not rock the Christian boat too much?

The brave madman Nietzsche pulled the plug on that polite hypocrisy. He yanked down the silk breeches of the eighteenth-century Deists. He pulled off their powdered wigs, exposed their highfalutin philosophizing, and spoke the truth.

God or Nothing

Nietzsche reserved his most vehement condemnation for the Christians who attempted to weave the Deism of their age into Christianity. He accused liberal biblical scholars such as David Strauss, who denied the supernatural dimension of the Faith, of not having the courage of their convictions.

These men were hypocrites of the first degree—keeping their pulpits and paychecks, their scholarships and their chairs of theology when all along, the end point of their polite materialism had to be atheism. There was no way around it. God was dead, and they had killed Him.

In *The Gay Science*, Nietzsche sets a scene in which a madman goes through the city streets in broad daylight shouting, "I seek God!... Where has God gone?... I mean to tell you! We have killed him, you and I. We are all his murderers!... Do we not hear the noise of grave diggers who are burying God? Do we not smell the divine putrefaction? For even Gods putrefy. God is dead! God remains dead and we have killed him."[10]

If materialism is a mask of atheism, it is also a mask of nihilism. If there is nothing but this physical world, then ultimately there is nothing at all, because you and I and all things will die and decay into dust, and "I will show you fear in a handful of dust."[11]

Puddleglum the Preacher

This is why I stand with Puddleglum. At the climax of *The Silver Chair*, the queen of the underworld casts a spell over Puddleglum, the prince, and the children. She sings a siren song and almost convinces them that there is no Narnia, there is no overworld where the sun shines and the sky is blue. Her enchantment almost works.

But then Puddleglum, the pessimistic realist, stamps out the fire that spreads the witch's intoxicating incense and says:

One word, Ma'am.... I won't deny any of what you said. But there's one thing more to be said, even so. Suppose we *have* only dreamed, or made up, all those things — trees and grass and sun and moon and stars and Aslan himself. Suppose we have. Then all I can say is that, in that case, the made-up things seem a good deal more important than the real ones. Suppose this black pit of a kingdom of yours

---

10 Friedrich Nietzsche, *The Gay Science*, quoted in Robert Cardinal Sarah, *God or Nothing* (San Francisco: Ignatius Press, 2015), 170.

11 T. S. Eliot, *The Waste Land: The Complete Poems and Plays* (New York: Harcourt, Brace and World, 1971), 38.

is the only world. Well, it strikes me as a pretty poor one. And that's a funny thing, when you come to think of it. We're just babies making up a game, if you're right. But four babies playing a game can make a play world which licks your real world hollow. That's why I'm going to stand by the play world. I'm on Aslan's side even if there isn't any Aslan to lead it. I'm going to live as like a Narnian as much as I can even if there isn't any Narnia."[12]

---

[12] Lewis, *The Silver Chair*, 158–159.

2

Angry Young Atheists

Scientism and Historicism

From time to time, I have allowed myself to be drawn into arguments on the Internet with angry young men who have watched too many YouTube videos.

The Internet atheist sticks out his chin and growls, "You believe in God? Where's your evidence. Huh?"

My response is to ask what sort of evidence he requires. Does he want me to produce the pitchfork the devil left behind, or would a hoofprint suffice? Does he want me to present a feather from the archangel Michael's wing so he can put it under a microscope to analyze its DNA? Does he wish for a photograph of the Resurrection? Well, there is always the Shroud of Turin.

Science is all about measurement and analysis of the physical realm. That's what science *is*, and thank God for it. What a wonderful world we enjoy because of the discoveries of science and the advances of technology! Asking for "evidence," however, reminds me of the cosmonaut who came back to earth and reported confidently that he did not see any angels or a big golden city up there. You can't photograph angels or do a chemical analysis of the pearls in the pearly gates. Every decent scientist would agree that science can have nothing to say about the existence of God, Heaven, Hell, or eternal life.

Looking for scientific evidence for the eternal realm is like taking apart an alarm clock to look for time.

Science and Religion

Nevertheless, an almost universal assumption in the modern world is that science has disproved religion. Did I say when you cut off one head of the Hydra, two more grow back? The obvious outgrowth of materialistic atheism is the third head of the Hydra: scientism.

Scientism "is the philosophical notion which refuses to admit the validity of forms of knowledge other than those of the positive sciences, and it relegates religious, theological, ethical and aesthetic knowledge to the realm of mere fantasy.... Scientism consigns all that has to do with the question of the meaning of life to the realm of the irrational or imaginary."[13]

The modern scientific method began to develop in the late Middle Ages, and the objective study of nature continued to develop through the Renaissance. However, it was during the Enlightenment of the eighteenth century that the study of nature divorced from the supernatural really exploded.

As the physical world became more intriguing, God became irrelevant. Then, in the nineteenth century, the followers of Charles Darwin suggested that perhaps God wasn't really involved in the natural order at all. The natural order just *was*, and nature changed and developed on its own at random through a mysterious dynamism called "life." As we shall see, this scientific theory has become one of the foundations of our modern worldview.

---

[13] Pope John Paul II, *Fides et Ratio: On the Relation between Faith and Reason* (Boston: Pauline Books and Media, 1998), 109–110.

Miracles and Mothman

What interests me, however, is that despite the widespread assumption that science has debunked religion, there seems to be more interest than ever in the paranormal. People may not believe in God, Jesus, Mary, and angels, but they are intrigued by Bigfoot, aliens, the Mothman, and the Loch Ness monster. They may not go to Mass, but they'll call on Madame Mim the fortune-teller. They may not pray the Rosary, but they'll play the Ouija board.

So, on the one hand, people assume that the material world is all there is, but they are heretics in the materialist church. Deep down, they really do believe in the invisible realm; they just don't believe in religion. This popular paradox pushes me to examine this twilight zone between the ordinary and the extraordinary. And this brings me to the topic of miracles, because if there *is* any kind of evidence for the supernatural realm, it would consist of some kind of interaction between the physical and nonphysical realms.

This is why, if I had magical powers, I would love to arrange a meeting between the Scottish philosopher David Hume (d. 1776) and St. Joseph Cupertino (d. 1663). Hume is famous for his denial of any metaphysical realities and his rejection of miracles. His essential argument is that, given the fixed laws of nature, miracles are so improbable as to be impossible. In other words, miracles can't happen because miracles are impossible.

With such circular reasoning and special pleading spinning in one's head, it would be interesting to take Mr. Hume on a flying visit (as it were) to St. Joseph Cupertino's friary in Italy. Joseph Cupertino was not nearly as clever as the intellectually brilliant David Hume. In fact, poor old Joseph was a dolt. He was very good at prayer, however, and experienced various mystical marvels, including the gift of levitation.

Beheading Hydra

So what would it be like to get David Hume to witness St. Joseph of Cupertino floating in the air and then ask what he thought about miracles? The conversation might go something like this:

BELIEVER IN MIRACLES. Look, Mr. Hume. Do you see Brother Joseph floating up there in the rafters?

DAVID HUME. I do indeed.

BIM. What do you make of that then, you Scottish scoffer?

DH. Och, to be sure, it's a marvel.

BIM. So you believe in miracles now, do you?

DH. I'm not so sure.

BIM. But there's a fellow floating up there! Surely that's a miracle. It completely breaks your unbreakable laws of nature.

DH. Perhaps not.

BIM. Come now. The law of gravity is pretty locked in, isn't it? Things don't float. Monks don't levitate, but here before you is a flying monk. How do you explain that? Suddenly your logical positivism is neither logical nor positive.

DH. Very witty, but I'm not actually a logical positivist. That comes later. I don't disagree. Brother Joseph there certainly seems to be levitating. It's a marvel and a mystery, to be sure, but I'm not convinced that it is a miracle.

BIM. It's not a miracle? How so?

DH. Well, you know it could be that it is simply the case that the law of gravitation is more complicated than we first thought. Perhaps built into the law of gravitation are some laws we have yet to understand that allow for the suspension of the law under certain conditions.

BIM. Help me here. It seems obvious to me that a flying monk is an example of a miracle.

DH. You would agree, would you not, that there is a law against killing a man?

BIM. Of course: thou shalt not kill.

DH. And yet we all understand that under certain conditions it is perfectly acceptable to kill a man.

BIM. In war, yes. In self-defense.

DH. So perhaps written within the law of gravitation are certain conditions within the greater natural order that we do not yet comprehend, that allow for the suspension of the laws of gravitation. Ye needn't posit the intervention of the Almighty. Besides, what point would there be anyway in Almighty God deciding that Brother Joseph ought to be floating about like a butterfly?[14]

You see how difficult it is to cut off a head of the Hydra?

Reality Is Rubbery

Miracles do happen, and what they reveal to us is that reality is rubbery. It is unpredictable. There is a strangeness to miracles that defies our human logic. Why, for example, should St. Bernadette's body have been incorrupt when they opened her coffin thirty years after her death, whereas the body of another saintly French nun who died young — St. Thérèse of Lisieux — was found to be reduced to the usual dust and bones?

---

[14] An excellent discussion of the relationship of the laws of nature to miracles is found in C. S. Lewis's essay "Religion without Dogma?"; it can be found in his collection of essays *God in the Dock: Essays on Theology and Ethics*, ed. Walter Hooper (Grand Rapids, MI: William B. Eerdmans, 1970).

Beheading Hydra

Miracles simply remind us that weird things happen. All sorts of odd and unexpected events take place for which science has no explanation. The David Humes of this world would retort, "This is what we call the 'God of the gaps.' When there is a gap in your scientific knowledge, you wheel in your divine miracle-worker. But as scientific knowledge advances, one by one those so-called miracles turn out to have natural explanations."

Not so fast. It is true that superstitious people assign natural wonders to supernatural forces. They say Mother Teresa's face appeared in a toasted bagel. No. It was just a toasted bagel, and we have a name for that sort of magic thinking. It's called pareidolia. Nevertheless, weird things happen. Friars float. Dead saints smell like flowers thirty years after they were buried. Seventy thousand people said they saw the sun spin and plummet to earth at Fatima.

Can miracles all be explained away, or do they prove the existence of the supernatural realm? In a way, they do prove the existence of the supernatural realm, but not perhaps in the way one expects. When a monk floats up to the ceiling, it could be the intervention of the deity helping the poor man to levitate, but it could also be, as I had David Hume say, that there are principles within the laws of nature that allow those laws to be suspended. But isn't that the definition of *supernatural*—above or greater than the laws of nature?

If we allow for the possibility of a Divine Creator—the one who set up the laws in the first place—then He must be able to interrupt the natural order if He wishes. It also makes sense that He created the natural order with a certain open-ended quality: with lacunae—gaps within the natural order where unexpected things can happen and where He can intervene. In other words, He created a porous, elastic universe.

It is the job of science to discover and document the laws of nature, but what science cannot do is discover or predict all the exceptions and variables in those laws. One can legislate and attempt to enforce traffic laws, for example, but no one can predict who will break the speed limit, run a red light, and crash into a telephone pole. In fact, the very nature of a law assumes that it is possible to break the law — or why would the law have been made in the first place?

It is the same with the laws of nature. They are made to be broken, and the only one who can break them is the one who made them. So experience would indicate that there are doorways, if you like, between worlds. There are interstices in the natural order through which the greater forces can enter. In other words, there is a fluid interaction between the natural order and a power that is greater than the natural order — a power that can surge through the gaps and create what we call a miracle.

What a Wonderful World

The spiritual person sees miracles — divine interruptions — all around him, in and through his everyday experience. He sees a constant interaction between this world and the next. They are a flourish, if you like — an ad lib by the divine actor or the improvisations that a top-rate musician might add to a Chopin prelude.

More importantly, the person of faith sees God's mighty hand working not only in and through nature but within the whole sweep of human history. As my hokey Sunday school teacher used to tell us, "History is 'His story.'"

That history is a roller coaster of triumphs and tragedies, but, within and through it all, the believer traces the intention and intervention of a loving God, who neither tramples on human freedom nor delivers humanity to the worst of our diabolical schemes.

The materialist atheist, however, denies this reality. Because there is no storyteller, there can be no story. History is therefore a jungle book—a series of brutal random events: a chronicle of the members of one tribe killing those of another, raping their women, enslaving their children, and burning their huts. Denying any overarching meaning to history is the fourth ism, and it is named Historicism.

Furthermore, because there is no storyteller—no beginning and no happy ending—the truths of any time period are merely the result of that particular epoch and culture. "The fundamental claim of historicism ... is that the truth of a philosophy is determined on the basis of its appropriateness to a certain period and a certain historical purpose. At least implicitly, therefore, the enduring validity of truth is denied. What was true in one period, historicists claim, may not be true in another."[15]

While the person of faith sees God at work through nature and through the great drama of history, the narrow-minded materialistic citizen of this world sees only the dull and predictable laws of nature and a sequence of human struggles for power. He is under the enchantment of the Green Queen. He sees no miracles or marvels. He sees no plan and no providence, and if presented with a miracle or a sign of God's action in human history, he will find a way to explain it away.

Remember, these isms are rarely consciously held opinions. They are the basic assumptions—the default setting in our modern atheistic society.

---

[15] Pope John Paul II, *Fides et Ratio*, no. 87.

Father Fraudulent

What is even more troubling is that this same miracle- and providence-denying mentality has taken root even among the Christian clergy.

For example, we have all come across the lame sermon about the feeding of the five thousand, in which the modernist preacher explains in hushed tones that "the *real* miracle is that everyone shared their lunch." Come now. The real miracle is that anybody believes such a stupid interpretation of what the Gospel clearly presents as an astounding miracle.

What is most disturbing is that this preacher will explain how Jesus' feeding of the five thousand, calming the storm, and walking on the water are myths conjured up by the early Christian community. He'll explain away the exorcisms as obvious cases of epilepsy and Jesus' healing miracles as psychosomatic illnesses that were "healed" as the person's self-esteem was raised.

And if all this is not silly enough, the same priest will go directly from the pulpit to recite the Nicene Creed, professing that Jesus Christ is "God from God, Light from Light ... begotten, not made, consubstantial with the Father," by whom all things were made. The same priest will stand up on Easter Day and with a straight face proclaim, "Christ is risen! He is risen indeed! Alleluia!" What a phony! What a fraud! How can the man deny the miracles of Jesus in the Gospels and then profess his belief in the even more astounding miracles of the Incarnation and the Resurrection? The fact is, he doesn't believe any of it. He's embarrassed by the historical Christian faith and has been conned into a fake version of Christianity by two hundred years of bogus scholarship and atheistic philosophy, and he has been bullied into odious hypocrisy by the blind followers of scientism and historicism — many of whom were his seminary professors.

Can we have a Christianity without miracles? C. S. Lewis writes:

> The one religion in the world ... with which you could not do that is Christianity. In a religion like Buddhism, if you took away the miracles attributed to Gautama Buddha ... there would be no loss. In fact, the religion would get along much better without them because ... the miracles largely contradict the teaching. Even in the case of Mohammedanism (Islam) nothing essential would be altered if you took away the miracles.... But you cannot possibly do that with Christianity, because the Christian story is precisely the story of one grand miracle, the Christian assertion being that what is beyond all space and time, what is uncreated, eternal came into nature—into human nature, descended into his own universe and rose again bringing nature up with him. It is precisely one great miracle. If you take that away there is nothing specifically Christian left.[16]

All or Nothing

So what is the right relationship between religion, science, and history? One does not prove or disprove the other. Instead, the natural and the supernatural world are interwoven. The Creator God is out there, but, by virtue of the Incarnation, He is also *in here*, acting within the natural world and human history. He is Emmanuel—God with us. We are destined to discover the wonders of the created order through science and history so that we might also discover with even more wonder the constant

---

[16] C. S. Lewis, "The Grand Miracle," in *God in the Dock*, 76.

action of the One who created such beauty and order and who devised a beautiful plan to redeem a fallen world.

You might ask why it matters. It matters because the first set of isms have to do with "the world." What we believe affects how we behave. In the next two chapters, we'll meet four more isms—four more heads of the Hydra that are the terrifying applications of materialism, atheism, scientism, and historicism that we can see woven in and through in the modern world.

3

Bring Me the Head of Jeremy Bentham

Utilitarianism and Pragmatism

Did you know that the atheist philosopher Jeremy Bentham (d. 1832) requested that, after he died, his body should be dissected, mummified, and put on display? It's true. After a public autopsy, his friends cut off his head with the intention of preserving it. The mummification of his body failed, so they boiled down Bentham's skeleton and then padded it out with straw—like some hideous scarecrow—and dressed it in his clothes.

The attempt to preserve his head, using techniques from cannibals of New Zealand, was not successful. The shrunken head was grotesque, so they put it in what looks like an old pickle jar and commissioned a wax effigy, stuck it on the padded-out skeleton, added some of Bentham's hair, and topped it off with a preposterous straw hat. This macabre display—like some ghastly parody of the effigies of saints you'll find in French churches—can be viewed in the student center of University College, London.

Materialism in Action

Bentham was the father of utilitarianism—the philosophy that whatever brings the greatest happiness to the greatest number of people must be the measure of what is good. When materialism and scientism put on their working clothes, you get utilitarianism—the fifth Hydra head that poisons modern society. Bentham was a radical atheist who wanted to abolish not only all religion but every thought of religion. His utilitarianism is rooted in the empiricism of David Hume, whom we met in the last chapter. Because of Bentham's disbelief (like Hume's) in anything other than this physical realm, it follows that it is a waste of time to be concerned with metaphysical or religious questions.

Being of a practical turn of mind, and given his basic assumptions, Bentham's utilitarian conclusions make sense: if there is nothing but this world, then let's make this world the best it can be. It is obvious that the way to make the world a better place is to make people happy, and whatever brings the most happiness to the most people must be best. There is a childlike naïveté to this so-called philosophy that would be charming if it weren't so insidious.

Although Bentham used the word *happiness*, he might just as well have used the word *pleasure*, for if he believed in nothing but this material realm, then happiness could only be happiness in this world, and happiness in this material world is clearly whatever brings one pleasure. Bentham didn't punch below the belt, as Freud would later with his theories about the pleasure principle, but pleasure must still be the siren beckoning beneath Bentham's call for universal happiness.

As with all of the heads of the Hydra, the concept of utilitarianism seems so simple and obvious that one can scarcely dare to challenge it. Surely it is crystal clear that the best thing is for the largest possible number of people to be happy. But as with the other heads of the Hydra, when you begin to apply some pressure and to probe, the problems appear.

Problems with the Happiness Hydra

If a toddler is screaming for a lollipop, it is obvious that his mother could make the child happy by giving him a lollipop. The problem is that too many lollipops will rot the child's teeth and he will soon have more pain than pleasure. Furthermore, by rewarding his screaming, his mother may be spoiling him and producing an adult who will never be happy unless he has a constant supply of sweet pleasures.

The child might assert his bellowing belligerence and win. His mother may give in and give him the lollipop. Alternatively, she might decide that, in the long run, it would be better (and more pleasurable) for the child not to receive a lollipop. In that way, he will begin to learn self-control and, through self-discipline, will become a better and therefore a happier person.

This simple illustration reveals the underlying problems with the utilitarian principle of seeking merely happiness. There are four basic problems with utilitarianism that begin with the letter *p*: personal taste, proportionality, pain, and power.

The first problem with the pleasure principle is personal taste. Who decides what happiness is? One man's pleasure is another man's pain. I like grand operas. You like soap operas. I like hot dogs. You like hors d'oeuvres. The brat liked yelling and lollipops. His mother liked silence and self-discipline. Who is to say what brings happiness, and what *is* happiness, after all?

I am happy when I am eating a huge meal with plenty of wine, but I am unhappy afterward when I have indigestion. Does happiness consist simply of having food, shelter, and security? I am happy that my job provides the money to pay my bills and keep my family in material comfort, but what if I loathe my boss, hate my job, and experience total misery for eight hours every day?

Beheading Hydra

Are we concerned only with physical happiness? What about peace of mind, self-esteem, the experience of beauty, or the love of family and friends? Even excluding the reality of the spiritual realm, might religious or spiritual happiness be included in the assessment? Who would judge such subjective aspects of happiness?

To be fair, the next generation of utilitarian, John Stuart Mill (whose father was good friends with Bentham), was subtler in his approach and understood that equating happiness merely with personal pleasure was problematic.

The Problem of Proportionality

The second problem with the happiness principle is proportionality. If we judge on pleasure alone, how do we judge what is most pleasant for the most people? Do we judge by the intensity of the pleasure, the duration of the pleasure, or simply by the number of people who seem to be happy?

Would base physical pleasures be lower and intellectual pleasures be higher? For example, would watching pornography be better than reading Plato? Is a long-lasting, mild happiness for five people better than a sublime but fleeting pleasure for five hundred? Are the pleasures of the mob really more important than the pleasures of the elite, or vice versa?

If we are seeking the greatest pleasure for the greatest number, then we must decide for the base vulgarities, not the Beatific Vision. But are the crude pleasures truly better than the sublime?

Surely not.

The problems of the proportionality of pleasure suddenly makes the whole process far more complex than we first imagined.

As Mill wrote, "It is quite compatible with the principle of utility to recognize the fact that some *kinds* of pleasure are more desirable and valuable than others. It would be absurd that, while estimating all other things quality is considered as well as quantity, the estimation of pleasure should be supposed to depend on quantity alone."[17]

Pain, Pleasure, and Power

Although one is grateful for Mill's balance, a third problem remains, and it is the problem of pain. Ironically, the pursuit of happiness invariably brings pain, and there is a universal wisdom that the greatest happiness involves the greatest pain.

I must practice for years and sacrifice all if I wish to play Rachmaninov's Third Piano Concerto. If I desire the exhilarating pleasure of standing on the top of Mount Everest, I must first go through months of training, the exhaustion and expense of the expedition, blisters, frostbite, and all the pain of climbing the mountain.

Furthermore, psychologists tell me that if I attempt to avoid all pain and pursue nothing but base pleasure, I will end up with nothing but pain. When a child eats too many lollipops, he gets a stomachache and tooth decay and has to go the dentist and endure great pain.

Therefore, the person who pursues nothing but pleasure either endures great pain to get that pleasure or ends up with great pain because he has chosen nothing but easy pleasure. Pleasure and pain are always mixed, and you cannot have one without the other, any more than you can have light without shadow. How, then, could anybody attempt to assess what real happiness consists of?

[17] John Stuart Mill, *Utilitariansim*, 7th ed. (London: Longmans, Green, 1879), chap. 2, Project Gutenberg, http://www.gutenberg.org/files/11224/11224-h/11224-h.htm.

Beheading Hydra

I went on a cruise once, and my complaint about it was that the staff were constantly trying to make me enjoy myself. This brings me to the fourth problem with the pleasure principle: power.

If one happiness is better than another, should it be imposed on a person who does not want that form of happiness? If it were imposed, would it still make him happy? Some people love being miserable. Shall we force them to be happy? Shall we have a Ministry of Happiness, in which scientists and educated bureaucrats research human happiness, decide what gives us the most pleasure, and then force this happiness on us? Will they vote on their findings?

To read Mill's more nuanced version of utilitarianism is hopeful, but sadly, that is not the philosophy that has prevailed in our modern society. Instead, we have an insistence on the pursuit of happiness, but it is a prescribed corporate happiness dreamed up by the pragmatic and politically correct. If "the greatest happiness for the greatest number" is the guiding principle, then someone must decide what will provide the most happiness for the greatest number, and that person must impose his idea of happiness on everyone else.

Mill sounds balanced, and Bentham sounds benevolent when he proposes happiness for everyone, but Bentham is Mill's master, and another of Bentham's guiding principles was this: "Nature has placed mankind under the governance of two sovereign masters, pain and pleasure. It is for them alone to point out what we ought to do, as well as to determine what we shall do. They govern us in all we do, in all we say, in all we think."[18]

Aha! Did he say pleasure *and* pain? That *both* are motivators? Then it must follow that the person who is offering pleasure for

---

[18] Jeremy Bentham, *Morals and Legislation*, chap. 1.

the large number of people must be willing to apply a negative sanction to those who are keeping the majority from achieving the fullness of happiness. It is a cheerful thought to be offered happiness. It is not so cheering to be encouraged to embrace that "happiness" with a stun gun, handcuffs, and free admission to a residential "re-education center."

Pragmatism and Practicality

No doubt if Jeremy Bentham were invited into the conversation, he would say, "I am not concerned with all your technicalities and philosophizing. My plan is not so insidious or as complicated as you think. I am merely proposing practical, commonsense solutions for various social issues, such as prison reform, economics, and education. This has nothing to do with your theology or metaphysical ideas of ethics."

This is exactly the problem, and it brings us to the sixth head of the Hydra. Pragmatism is an offshoot of utilitarianism, with a subtle difference in emphasis. Pope John Paul II defined *pragmatism* as "an attitude of mind which, in making its choices, precludes theoretical considerations or judgments based on ethical principles."[19] In other words, in addition to making people happy, we should do so in the most practical, efficient, and cost-effective way possible, and there needn't be any other ethical, religious, or moral considerations.

For instance, is fifteen-year-old Sally suddenly pregnant after a happy experience at a party with her sixteen-year-old boyfriend, Tommy? Never mind. Let's find the greatest happiness for the largest number of people, and let's do that as quickly, efficiently, and cheaply as possible. Sally can't have a baby at her age, and

---

[19] Pope John Paul II, *Fides et Ratio*, no. 89.

Tommy is not prepared to be a husband and father. Let's whisk Sally off to the abortion clinic.

When Granny is in a nursing home, having lost her marbles, and lies in bed drooling all day, what shall we decide? The utilitarian pragmatist argues that Granny has no real quality of life. She's not happy. She demands constant care, and that's expensive.

Is it not more merciful (and cheaper) simply to assist Granny on her "final journey"? says the pragmatist. She will die soon anyway. Is it not better for the rest of the family—indeed, for the rest of society—to give Granny some medicine so she will just go to sleep ... and not wake up?

When pragmatic solutions are seen at the personal level, the ultimate cruelty of the philosophy is understood. More chillingly, it should be understood that the utilitarian pragmatist does not see himself as cruel. Indeed, he always veils his cruelty with the euphemisms of kindness.

Do you think I am being extreme and that this behavior is not already with us? You are deceiving yourself. Utilitarian pragmatism is woven through the fabric of our modern society. It is everywhere. It is the atmosphere we breathe in this society that so values "life, liberty, and the pursuit of happiness."

The Pragmatic Pastor

Just as scientism and historicism have infected the Christian church, so utilitarianism and pragmatism have poisoned our pastors. The clergyman who denies miracles invariably takes a utilitarian and pragmatic view of the Christian religion. This follows from his underlying materialistic understanding. Once he has ruled out the miraculous, what is left of religion? Just a set of rules for respectability. This isn't religion. This is Girl Scouts selling cookies.

Religion has always been about an encounter with the other side. Whether it is a caveman worshipping a cow or a shaman conjuring up a daemon; whether it is a holy priest in contemplation or a Buddhist monk with his prayer beads and begging bowl; whether it is an old lady muttering her Rosary, a missionary embracing a leper, or a martyr climbing the scaffold, religion has been about an adventurous excursion into the invisible realm.

The modernist Christian, on the other hand, has shot down the angels in full flight and cast out all the demons in the name of Jeremy Bentham. Rather than preparing souls for a better place, the utilitarians have turned the Christian religion into a method for making the world a better place. In 2005, religious researchers Melinda Lundquist Denton and Christian Smith dubbed this false religion "moralistic therapeutic deism." This is a "Christianity" that is no more than a collection of rules for respectability and some techniques for helping with personal problems, hitched to a vague spirituality. Instead of an encounter with the living God, this religion is a nauseating gathering of navel-gazing, politically correct do-gooders. No wonder people stay away.

I hate this false religion with a holy hatred. Utilitarian Christianity is not Christianity at all, and anyone from the highest prelate to the lowest pew sitter who pulls the plug on the Holy Spirit and turns Christianity into no more than a system of morality and therapy, or teaches that saving the rainforest is more important than savings souls, will be cast into the outer darkness where there is weeping and wailing and the gnashing of teeth (see Matt. 8:12).

It's not surprising, therefore, that a utilitarian church has also been infected with pragmatism. The insurance men, the financiers, the public-relations people, and the lawyers run the show. Our parishes and dioceses are run like corporations, with the human resources departments sending out memos and creating regulations to ensure that nobody will ever be sued, that everyone's health-care plan is in place, that their pensions are secure, and that all the toilets are working. You thought we were to walk by faith and not by sight? The pragmatist Christians would tell you not to be naïve and to make sure you've completed all your paperwork.

Self-Righteous Liars

The most noxious thing about the utilitarian do-gooders is that they believe they are delightful people. Remember, not only is the pragmatist doing something good, but he sees himself as doing something noble for the greater and higher cause of "the greatest happiness for the greatest number."

Enter the eugenicist. The masters of the master race are the ultimate utilitarians. Intent on purifying humanity of "the people we don't want more of," the eugenicists and abortionists don't want just ethnic cleansing: they want to cleanse the whole human race.

Any concerns for the individual are ultimately irrelevant because the ideology of the eugenicist is built on a foundation of materialism. The utilitarian eugenicist does not believe in the eternal soul; therefore, he does not believe in the value of each individual. As far as he is concerned, like all the Margaret Sangers of this world, he is merely sending the victims to oblivion. Eliminating the unborn, the unfit, the disabled, the elderly, or the ethnically inferior is no worse than pulling weeds or exterminating rats. Furthermore, since the genocidal utilitarian does not believe in an afterlife, he has no fear about his own destiny. He believes that, when his time comes, he, too, will simply cease to exist. That being the case, he will never have to answer for his crimes.

This is why the gruesome head of Jeremy Bentham is such an ironically appropriate symbol. His shrunken head stands for the thousands of heads severed by Madame Guillotine in the Reign of Terror — which, of course, aimed to bring about the greatest good for the greatest number of people. Bentham's severed head stands as a symbol of all those who were herded into the gas chambers in order to bring about the wonderful happiness of a master race for the German people. His head stands for the Christians beheaded by Islamic radicals who pray for a great caliphate in which everyone will at last be happy. Bentham's head stands for the ideas behind the millions imprisoned, tortured, shot, and starved by the communist and socialist regimes across the globe that were all going to make everyone so wonderfully and everlastingly happy.

So bring me the head of Jeremy Bentham, and let me hold it aloft as a grim and gruesome warning.

4

O Brave New Disneyworld

Progressivism and Utopianism

While living in the United Kingdom, I observed a curious difference between the New World and Merry Old England. Their advertising was different.

In America, we were constantly told that a product was "new and improved." More scoops of raisins were forever being added to the raisin bran. The peanut butter was always crunchier than ever. Every year, the cars were sleeker, safer, and more luxurious, had more gadgets, *and* were cheaper to buy. Nearly everything, from sandwiches to skyscrapers, was constantly being updated, improved, renovated, and restyled. New was always better.

In the Old Country, it was the reverse. Rather than advertising a product as "new and improved," it was likely to be billed as "old-fashioned." Labels were printed in "Ye Olde English" style. Traditional British images of Big Ben, Tower Bridge, crowns, and coronets were everywhere. If you want to sell something in England, put it in a tin box with a picture of a thatched cottage on the front.

One of the favorite advertising tricks was to get a royal warrant for your product. If Her Majesty the Queen would only purchase your waxed jacket, your marmalade, shoe polish, or pickles, you could print the royal coat of arms on your label, and (let's say you produced axes) you could brag, "Purveyors of fine cutlery to the Royal Executioner since the reign of Henry VIII."

When I lived in the damp lands, the English seemed to be suspicious of progress, and my instinct is to be on their side. I like old-fashioned better. The idea that something is good or bad merely because it is new or old, however, is ridiculous. The basic assumption in the modern world that *progress* is both inevitable and good is the seventh head of the Hydra, and I'm afraid that even the English have been seduced by the concept. The fact that they are building skyscrapers that tower over Ye Olde Cheddar Cheese[20] proves my point.

Progress or Progressivism?

Like the other isms, progressivism is not a belief that is stated explicitly, nor does anyone attempt to undermine it. Whether it is the field of medicine, domestic comfort, transportation, entertainment, or technology, we simply assume that *new* must mean "improved" and therefore "better."

It's pretty hard to avoid that conclusion because we really have made progress — especially over the last hundred years.[21] To give just a sampling: Worldwide infant mortality is plummeting. Maternal survival of childbirth is zooming upward. Abject

---

20 Ye Olde Cheddar Cheese was a pokey little London pub beloved of G. K. Chesterton.

21 See Marian L. Tupy, "Human Progress: Not Inevitable, Uneven, and Indisputable," Cato Institute, October 30, 2013, https://www.cato.org/publications/commentary/human-progress-not-inevitable-uneven-indisputable.

poverty is disappearing. More people than ever are literate and receiving higher education. More people have access to electricity, clean water, computers, and the Internet. Fewer people live under dictatorships. More people can travel and enjoy freedom and democracy. Despite the claims of environmentalists, the water and air quality worldwide are better than they have been for decades. Because of medical advances, more diseases are being eradicated for more people worldwide. People live longer, experience less pain, and enjoy a better quality of life for longer than ever before.

So, you might ask, why you are you being such a party pooper? Look at all the good things science, technology, and progress have brought us!

But to poop on your party, I should point out that the last hundred years have also brought us a long list of other things that were new: Auschwitz was new. Communism, the Gulag, the enslavement of Eastern Europe, Stalin's starvation of the Ukrainians, Mao's slaughter of millions, the killing fields of Cambodia. The atom bomb, millions of unborn killed through abortion, the sale of body parts of dead babies, genetic engineering, Internet pornography, gender reassignment surgery for teens: all of these, and so much more, were new.

We may be enjoying unparalleled individual freedom, health, wealth, and opportunity in our society, but broken homes, loneliness, alcoholism and drug addiction, and suicides have also skyrocketed.

It's obvious, then, that just because something is new, that does not mean it is good. Just as we don't have a problem with science, but we do have a problem with the ideology of scientism, so we don't have a problem with progress, but we do have a problem with the ideology of progressivism.

Beheading Hydra

The Myth of Progress

The idea that progress is always good springs from the Enlightenment thinkers of the eighteenth century. Voltaire (d. 1778) believed that science and rationalism would inevitably bring about material progress. Immanuel Kant (d. 1804) was less optimistic but believed that humanity was involved in a long, gradual struggle upward.

The philosopher Hegel (d. 1831) saw progress in terms of a struggle between opposing forces. There was a proposal—what he called a "thesis." This was countered by an opposing idea—the "antithesis." The advocates of the antithesis clashed with the proponents of the thesis, and out of the conflict came a new solution—a "synthesis."

Later in the nineteenth century, Charles Darwin (d. 1882) applied Hegel's ideas to his observations in the natural world. The fittest survived the clash of species. The English thinker Herbert Spencer (d. 1903) grabbed the baton from Darwin and ran with it. He applied Darwin's ideas on evolution to human society. Spencer saw the theory of evolution as a model for a great, inevitable ascent not only in the natural world but also in the human mind, culture, and history.

According to progressives, this clash within nature and human society is inevitable and (despite some pain) is always creative and positive. Furthermore, true progressives believe that it is legitimate to create the clash intentionally in order to bring about the synthesis (the desired new order) because the clash is natural, and the synthesis that comes out of the clash is always new, and that's "progress"—and progress is always good, right?

This assumption accounts for the unbelievably naïve and resilient optimism among progressives. They may witness umpteen revolutions and racks, guillotines, gas chambers, gulags, imposed famines, torture chambers, and firing squads, but they shrug their shoulders. "It's just the survival of the fittest. That's the way nature works. It's okay. There are some bumps in the road, but we're always moving onward and upward!" If you stand in the road when the progress bus is hurtling toward you, don't be surprised if you get run over. Hard luck!

This also explains why leftist progressives turn a blind eye to the riots, arson, threats, and violent protests of left-wing activists but clamp down on peaceful right-wing protests. The leftists see themselves as pioneers pushing for progress. The right wing are negative reactionaries who want to turn back the clock. Progressives are "good" even when they are violent and murderous. Conservatives are "bad" even when they are peaceful and prayerful.

If a myth is a fantasy story that gives meaning to the world, then this is the myth of progressivism. Notice also how this myth is a substitute for belief in divine providence. Instead of history being "His story"—instead of seeing God's mighty hand in all His works—the overarching story of progressivism is that of the noble upward surge of humanity forever driven forward by the mysterious forces of life itself!

Progressivism is a complicated lie interwoven and derived from the other heads of the Hydra, and like the others, it is the air we breathe. It is an assumed foundation of our society.

Progressive Priests

As with the other heads of the Hydra, you can tell the false religion because the priests push progressivism. The poison of progressivism in the Church is linked with the idea that truth is a product of a particular culture and time period, and it must adapt to different cultures and times accordingly.

This is why trendy Jesuit priests can suggest that the Scriptural prohibitions on homosexual activity were for that time, but "we know more about human sexuality now, and we should move on." In matters of both morality and doctrine, the progressive believes that the Church not only can change but *must* move forward with the great forward flow of history, and if this means being an activist and pushing for change, that's a noble part of being a disciple of Jesus. "His disciples were pioneers," progressives claim, "daring to step out to bring a new humanity into being."

The progressive priests also push for new ecumenical and interfaith understandings. They see humanity moving toward some great "Omega point" where our spiritual evolution as a race will be complete and we will all attain to the godhead within.[22]

Brave New Disneyworld

I've joked that America is one great conspiracy to make you happy, and there is no place that sums up the dream and the drive for happiness than Disneyworld. The Magic Kingdom stands as a symbol of all that is wonderful and happy for all. In all its pristine wholesomeness, Disneyworld seemingly combines fun, family values, harmless entertainment, and education with truth, justice, and the American way.

When I was living in England, the local aristocrat decided to take his family on vacation to Disneyworld. This surprised me because he was the sort of fellow who, I imagined, went to Scotland on vacation, camped out in the family castle, and tromped across the moors in tweeds and welly boots to shoot grouse before

---

[22] Ross Douthat gives a detailed critique of this wacky religion in chapter 7 of his book *Bad Religion*.

heading home to change into his kilt, sporran, and those knee socks with little knives in them. But no, he was headed off to Fantasyland. On their return, I asked Lord Blythering what he thought of Disneyworld.

He lifted an eyebrow, took a sip of his sherry, and said, "It's amazing what you Yanks can do with plastic."

Like all good jokes, it reveals the truth. Disneyworld—as a symbol of every Utopia mankind has ever dreamed up, is plastic. It's artificial. It's not real. St. Thomas More was the first to play with this idea with a pun. He wrote the book *Utopia*, and the word means both "good place" and "no place."

So why do we, despite all the dystopic novels and movies, still have such a hankering after utopias? Why, after the crushing horrors of communism and socialism, do we still fall for the plastic promises of the social engineers? Whether it is the call on the small scale of some dreamy religious cult, or a large-scale national or international plan for a global utopia, what is this strange, human obsession with not only making the world a better place but making the world a perfect place?

Progress toward Utopia

Utopianism, the eighth Hydra head, is a direct product of the first five isms.

If utilitarianism is the practical theory that comes from materialism and scientism, then utopianism is utilitarianism in action. Utilitarianism (because it is a practical theory) longs to be activated and fulfilled. "The greatest happiness for the greatest number" demands a society in which direct action is taken to ensure the greatest happiness for the greatest number.

A master plan must be devised, and it must be put in place as soon as possible because life is short. "Everyone will be happy when we have established communism. Don't you understand? Everyone will be happy when the master race is established and our nation is great again. Everyone *will* be happy. Do you hear me? And if you refuse to be happy, we will take you out and shoot you, and that will mean there are fewer unhappy people, and that means more happy people."

As Albert Camus observed, "The welfare of humanity is always the alibi of tyrants."[23]

The Tyranny of Happiness

Consequently, as history shows, utopianism must lead to tyranny. The utopian dreamers always wish to bring about the greatest good for the greatest number, but in the process, they will have no qualms about using arrest, imprisonment, torture, and murder to compel the lesser number.

It is easy to condemn Nazism and communism — the obviously utopian regimes of the twentieth century — while overlooking the utopianism that is an assumed aspect of American twenty-first-century life. The key point to remember about all these heads of the Hydra is that they are the foundation of our present society. They are already firmly in place. They are the air we breathe. They are not part of the culture. They *are* the culture, and all of us participate even when we dislike what is going on.

As Americans, we pride ourselves on individual freedoms, but think how our freedoms have already been whittled away by powers that are driven by the low-level utopianism that dreams of "life, liberty, and the pursuit of happiness." We have handed

[23] "Homage to an Exile" (1955), in Albert Camus, *Resistance, Rebellion, Death*, trans. Justin O'Brien (New York: Alfred A. Knopf, 1961), 101.

our children over to them to be educated. We have handed our money over to them through the financial services and insurance industry. They control the flow of information and shamelessly censor and manipulate the news cycle. They bombard us with their propaganda through advertising, education, publications, and social media. Already we are afraid of them, and our freedoms have not been taken from us as much as we have yielded them without a bleat of protest.

In an essay on the possibility of progress, C. S. Lewis observes, "The modern state exists not to protect our rights but to do us good or to make us good—anyway, to do something to us or make us into something. Hence the new name 'leaders' for those who were once 'rulers'. We are less their subjects than their wards, pupils or domestic animals. There is nothing left of which we can say to them, 'Mind your own business.' Our whole lives are their business."[24]

Creeping Utopia

The utopian plans for the future are unlikely to be introduced through a radical, violent social upheaval like the French, Russian, or Chinese revolutions. The new utopia is also unlikely to involve an omnipresent military, an oppressive secret police, or a uniformed nationalistic leader.

Instead, the next utopia will simply be a new way of life—a "new world order," if you like. It will be a living fulfillment of all of the isms. Being totally materialistic, it will be completely interlocked with science and technology. It will guarantee the greatest happiness to the greatest number of people through progress and pragmatic solutions. Moral considerations will not

[24] C. S. Lewis, "Is Progress Possible?," in *God in the Dock*, 349–350.

apply, and resistance will be futile because it will seem absurd. Why would anyone want to resist universal happiness?

A large proportion of Christians will be complicit in this seemingly benign utopianism. The false church of moralistic therapeutic deism already glides along with the utopian ideal. "This watered down, anemic, insipid form of Judeo-Christianity is pretty repulsive," writes Damon Linker, "but politically speaking, it's perfect: thoroughly anodyne, inoffensive, tolerant ... and perfectly suited to serve as the civil religion of the highly differentiated twenty-first century United States."[25]

This is what I call a creeping utopia or totalitarianism by stealth. If this creeping utopia is given a long enough run, armed revolution will be unnecessary. Religion will not have to be abolished because the nice, false religion of moralistic therapeutic deism will not be offensive to anyone. There will be no need for a civil war. The frog will be boiled by turning the heat up slowly, and the utopia achieved will last longer and be more effective because nobody will have realized it was taking over. Furthermore, the vast majority of people will be more than happy to be enslaved because being happy was what it was all about all along. Right?

As the noose of totalitarianism tightens, few will dare to speak against it. Why would anyone in his right mind be so nasty and insane as to criticize this brave new Disneyworld? How could anyone be unhappy at Disneyworld? Disneyworld was designed to make you happy. Don't you know?

---

[25] Damon Linker, "The Future of Christian America," *New Republic*, April 7, 2009, https://newrepublic.com/article/48917/the-future-christian-america.

The Flesh

When Satan tempted Jesus to turn stones to bread, he was attempting to get Jesus Christ to give in to His personal, physical desires.

This section of four isms underlying our modern world has to do with the temptations to individual souls. "The flesh" is not only the obvious "sins of the flesh," such as lust, gluttony, and sloth; to live according to the flesh is to have an unquestioned, personal, materialistic outlook, philosophy, and behavior.

5

The Gumby Men

Relativism and Indifferentism

When I was a child, there was a television character called Gumby. He was a chunky, rubbery stick figure who embarked on various adventures. Gumby existed not only in the kids' TV show. There were Gumby toys made of rubber over a wire armature, so you could bend Gumby into just about every posture imaginable. Gumby was a rubbery green contortionist.

I thought of Gumby when hearing a conversation not long ago between two Christian ladies who were debating the issue of same-sex "marriage." At the end of the discussion, the woman who was in favor of same-sex "marriage" smiled politely at her opponent and said, "Well, let's agree to disagree. You have your truth, and I have mine."

Of course, it is perfectly possible for two people to agree to disagree and still be friends, and it is also possible for there to be sincere differences of opinions on particular issues, but it is impossible for two opposite opinions both to be true. The woman's assertion, "You have your truth, and I have mine" is itself untrue.

Such intellectual contortions and logical impossibilities illustrate the fact that we now live in a population of Gumby men and women — rubbery individuals who have no established set of beliefs, religious tradition, philosophy of life, or systematic worldview.

Consequently, the Gumby people bend with whatever seems to be the majority opinion, the latest headline, peer pressure, or their present emotional state. As St. Paul put it, they are "tossed by waves and swept along by every wind of teaching" (Eph. 4:14). This lax and lackadaisical state of affairs may seem perfectly harmless, but as we go on, you'll see why it is, in fact, horribly harmful.

Dogma Must Go

The woman who said, "You have your truth, and I have mine" was giving popular expression to the ninth head of the Hydra: relativism. Put simply, relativism is the view that there is no such thing as truth, or if there is, it is impossible to state that truth in any completely clear way. Truth (if there is such a thing) is the product of particular cultures and circumstances.

According to the relativist, "truth" not only varies according to the cultures and circumstances in which it originated; it is also constantly shifting. As circumstances and cultures change, so our understanding and expression of "truth" changes.

Furthermore, because of progressivism, the relativist considers this to be a good thing. "Truth" is not just changing; it is changing for the better. Unchanging truth, on the other hand, cannot exist. Furthermore, as far as the relativist is concerned, dogma — that is, an unchanging, God-given statement of truth — is therefore not only unthinkable but dangerous.

R. R. Reno's book *The Return of the Strong Gods* catalogues the concerted effort by philosophers, political thinkers, economists, and theologians after the Second World War to exterminate dogma. They looked at the legacy of war, revolution, and political chaos in Western culture over the last five hundred years and concluded that the chaos was caused by people fighting over dogma—political ideologies and economic dogma, but most of all *religious* dogma.

To establish peace, they decided, dogma must go. Their theory did not come out of nowhere. When you look at philosophical development over the last five hundred years, everything was going in that direction anyway. Materialism gave way to scientism and empiricism, which gave way to deism, which yielded to atheism. It was a slam dunk. Relativism must follow from atheism. If there is no invisible dimension to reality, then there could be no God, and if there is no God, then it's obvious: there could be no divinely revealed dogma.

Furthermore, if there was no divinely revealed religious dogma, then a God-given moral code was also no more than a cultural phenomenon—a human invention. The anthropologists and students of comparable religion came to conclusions that complemented the idea. As they studied the array of world cultures, they concluded that all religions, with their strange myths, superstitions, rituals, dogmas, and moral codes, were merely humanly invented cultural artifacts and that Christianity was just one among many.

Religion without Dogma?

Christian theologians also jumped on the "let's get rid of dogma" train. In addition to Protestant theologians, Reno shows how Catholic theologian Karl Rahner pioneered a dogma-free "anonymous Christianity" in which atheists and nonbelievers could be saved because they were well-intentioned, nice people. Along with this warm, fuzzy theology, there was a new openness, reaching out to the marginalized, "breaking down barriers and overcoming binaries."[26]

These trends sat comfortably with the emerging ecumenical and interfaith movement in the second half of the twentieth century. If the dogma could be dumped, the divides could be bridged. The Christian ecumenists realized that getting rid of dogma completely would not fly, so (remembering that dogma came only out of particular historical circumstances and culture anyway) they determined that the dogma would be "reinterpreted" for a modern age.

Dogma-Free Catholicism?

This de-emphasis on dogma is clear in the motivation for the Second Vatican Council. Instead of "dogma that divides," the emphasis would be on the pastoral. Catholic theologians and prelates did not deny Catholic dogma. Instead, they stressed the pastoral application of Catholic beliefs and reminded everyone that the particular applications in different cultures and different circumstances would reflect "pastoral sensitivities."

The "pastoral approach" explains the present pope's ambiguity on doctrinal matters. Pope Francis has never denied Catholic dogma — but sometimes he declines to teach or preach it.

The typical modernist approach, therefore, was not to *deny* dogma but to reinterpret it in such a way that it would be acceptable not only to all Christians but, as much as possible, to all people. Whereas Catholics once understood church unity to be an invitation to Protestants to "come home to Rome," now ecumenism consisted of an agreed understanding of the

---

[26] R. R. Reno, *Return of the Strong Gods* (Washington, DC: Regnery Gateway, 2019), Kindle ed.

reinterpreted Catholic dogmas—and this introduces the tenth head of the Hydra: indifferentism.

Indifferentism is the logical conclusion of relativism in religion. Put simply, it is the idea that every Christian denomination is just a different expression of the same religion and that every religion is of equal value. The indifferent Christian cries, "Surely all that matters is how much we love Jesus!" And the interfaith enthusiast chirps, "We are all climbing the same mountain but on different paths; and as we climb that mountain, all the paths converge."

One Christian may well love Jesus more than another; however, it is patent nonsense that all Christian denominations are of equal value. Catholicism is far richer in every aspect: philosophy, spirituality, culture, art, architecture, history, and music. No matter what one's prejudices are, it is historically and objectively true that Catholicism is the richest and fullest expression of Christianity. Bob the Baptist may very well be a good Christian man who loves Jesus, but his religion is a truncated and inferior form of Catholicism, from which it is derived.

Likewise, it is nonsense to say that all religions are of equal value. Some religions are superior to others. Chartres Cathedral is not on a par with some squalid voodoo hut. Shall we compare Michelangelo's *Pietà* to Kali the Destroyer, and must we pretend that the terrifying religion of the Aztecs is as sublime as a Mozart Mass? Shall we equate the Sistine Chapel with your local megachurch in a renovated supermarket? Is an Alabama snake handler gospel meeting on a par with choral evensong in Kings College, Cambridge? I think not.

Indifferentism in religion serves only to weaken all religion, for when the dogma and the distinctive devotions go, all we are left with is vanilla spirituality. This is not a case of the blind leading the blind, but the bland leading the bland.

Beheading Hydra

Overweight Materialism

In his 1946 essay "Religion without Dogma?," C. S. Lewis analyzes the fatal flaw of indifferentism and relativist religion. As he does, he also unlocks the underlying problem of the whole relativistic mindset on which the rejection of dogma rests.

Dogma is impossible, argues the materialist, because there is no God to reveal the dogma. Religious truths are mere human inventions—the product of human thought. In fact, the thoroughgoing materialist must maintain that not only religious ideas are human inventions but that *all* ideas, moral precepts, and philosophical concepts can be no more than human inventions. This leads us to ask, "If all ideas are mere human inventions, where do the ideas come from? In other words, where does thought *itself* originate?

If there is only this material world, then thoughts and ideas are no more than chemical reactions in the brain as it processes data from the senses. Lewis asks how the human brain has this capacity. If the whole natural order is nothing more than a series of complex, irrational, random biological interactions (as the materialist holds), then the human brain is no more than a highly evolved, very complicated meaty computer. If materialism is true (and nature is no more than a result of random chemical reactions), then the human brain itself is no more than the result of random, irrational processes.

Lewis writes:

> Every particular thought ... is always and by all men discounted the moment they believe that it can be explained as the result of irrational causes. Whenever you know what the other man is saying is wholly due to his complexes or to a bit of bone pressing on his brain, you cease to attach

any importance to it. But if [materialism] were true, then all thoughts would be merely the result of irrational causes. Therefore all thoughts would be equally worthless. Therefore [materialism] is worthless. If it is true, we can know no truths. It cuts its own throat.[27]

The same is true of relativism. If the idea that "there is no such thing as truth" comes from the human brain, and if the human brain is the result of random, irrational evolution, then the statement "there's no such thing as truth" is also senseless.

But of course we know certain statements are true not because they are true in the realm of ideas but because, first of all, they are true in this physical world of reality. The philosopher proves the brick is real by kicking it and howling in pain.

The Scandal of Particularity

Another term for kicking the brick is "the scandal of particularity." This theological jargon refers to the intellectual scandal caused by the Incarnation of our Lord Jesus Christ. Put simply, it is intellectually respectable to be a Deist—to believe in the "the Creator." It is also intellectually respectable to believe in God as "the Force" or "the cosmic energy." (Star Wars is a very respectable religion.) This sort of god does what a god would do if you were inventing a religion. He remains where he belongs—up there in the spiritual realm. In other words, he remains an idea, a concept, a philosophical theory, or an energy field.

But have you ever tried to imagine this great energy force—this spiritual being that flows in and through all things? When I try to imagine this, all I come up with are images of strobe lights

---

[27] Lewis, "Religion without Dogma?," 144.

and electric current or else, as C. S. Lewis put it, "some vast tapioca pudding" in the sky.[28] We're physical beings. We have trouble trying to have a relationship with a vast tapioca pudding in the sky. We want particularity—something we can handle.

It is the cornerstone of the Christian religion that this vast tapioca pudding, this energy force, was also the Creator—the God of Abraham, Isaac, and Jacob; and He was their God because He got involved in their lives. He was in a relationship with a particular tribe of nomads in the Arabian desert and then deemed to descend into human history and take human flesh of a peasant girl in Nazareth before going on to teach the truth, heal people, and deliver them from bondage by dying and rising again to return to the invisible realm.

This is the "scandal of particularity." It's embarrassing. It's incredible. It's not intellectually respectable. Philosophers don't like it. To think that the one God—the majestic Creator, the Divine Architect, the Great Father of All—should become a mewling man-child! To think that He would come into a particular stable in a particular town in a particular province of a particular empire at a particular time on a particular day and that He would live a particular life and die on a particular Cross on a particular hillside outside a particular city on a particular Friday afternoon!

It's a scandal.

And yet, isn't particularity necessary for any idea, thought, or concept to become real? A Chopin nocturne becomes real only when it is recorded on particular notepaper and then played by a particular body seated at a particular piano with particular fingers hitting particular ivory keys that strike particular steel wires to

---

[28] C. S. Lewis, *Miracles: A Preliminary Study* (London: Geoffrey Bles, 1947), 90.

make particular sound waves that vibrate in particular eardrums of particular people.

An idea, thought, or concept is real only when it becomes particular, and the Christian religion is real only because of the scandal of the particularity of the Incarnation. God became man in place and time. In doing so, God became real. He was no longer a theory; He was a scandal of flesh and blood.

It is this same particularity that reveals the ridiculousness of relativism because relativism, by its very nature, can never be particular and therefore can never be real.

Furthermore, it is this particularity that demands not only a dogmatic religion but a sacramental one. The religion of the Incarnation must be dogmatic and sacramental because, like the Incarnation, it is real. It must therefore be solid. It must be historical. It must be experienced. It is not just a theory.

Indifferentism must fall in the face of these particular demands. The more real a religion becomes, the more particular it becomes and the more — by that very reality — it must be defined and specified; and the more it is defined and specified, the more it must exclude that which is outside the definition and particularity.

Terrifying Relativism

This is why authentic Christianity repudiates relativism and indifferentism, and it does so not with intellectual argumentation but with something called reality.

Relativism, by definition, is unreal. It has no definition. It is amorphous, vague, and impossible to pin down. If you should try to counteract the ordinary relativist with an argument based on truth, he will twist and slip-slide away. Even if he wishes to argue, he cannot do so, because his mind does not operate in a world where truth is possible. Arguing with a relativist is like wrestling with an octopus in oil in the dark.

It might seem as if an existence without the framework of truth is one of freedom, but the frightening reality is that mankind cannot live for very long without truth. When times are good and the sky is blue, the tolerant attitude that comes with relativism seems as if it will last forever. But beneath the surface, the Gumby people are restless and resentful—never satisfied and always searching. Beneath their empty minds and hearts there lurks another serpentine head—that of a deep, dark, nameless, chthonic fear.

The reason relativism is so terrifying is that when a whole population lives in an atmosphere where there is no truth, we do not have a society that is neutral. We have a society where there is no truth, and where there is no truth, there is not simply an empty space: there are lies.

Where the assumption is that there is no truth, people will lie. The media masters will lie. The advertising experts will lie. The educators will lie. The politicians will lie. The financial experts will lie. The people will lie. You will lie. Your neighbor will lie. Your spouse will lie. They will become the people of the lie.

In a society with no truth, no one can be trusted, and even worse, people will believe every lie that comes along. Not only will they believe the lies; they will attack anyone who dares even to suggest that the lies are lies.

Furthermore, in a society without truth, the people will be desperate for truth. They cannot live for long totally awash with lies swirling about them. They will be desperate for something to cling to. They will be desperate for a person to speak the truth to them. They will be desperate for a leader who promises to give them certainty and something, someone, in whom to believe.

The leader will give them what they long for. He will give them his "truth," and it will be propaganda—a carefully prepared and beautifully marketed compendium of lies.

And everyone who was taught that there is no truth will suck up this new "truth" from their new master. They will suck up this "truth" like thirsty people lost in the desert. They will regard this master as a person adrift in a lifeboat cries out with joy at the sight of a lighthouse.

But their new Master will be the antichrist, and they will be his willing slaves, and they will sell their souls and worship him.

6

Frank Sinatra Philosophy

Individualism and Tribalism

Fr. Paul—a friend of mine who is a vicar in England—informed me that the most popular song to be played at funerals in England is Frank Sinatra's "My Way."

You should understand that many English funerals take place in the government-run crematorium chapels. These are rather bleak municipal structures decorated with neutral religious symbols. There is a lectern, a simple cross, and a dais where the coffin is placed. When the officiating minister presses a button on the lectern, the crematorium employee plays the chosen recorded music.

To assist the bereaved to attain closure, when he chooses, the minister will then press another button. At that point, a machine behind the scenes whirs and a purple curtain glides out to veil the coffin from the congregation.

Fr. Paul always brings a heightened sense of drama to his celebration of the liturgy, so with an impish grin he informed me that if the family chooses Frank Sinatra's anthem to individualism, he plays the song and then waits to hit the second button until Ol' Blue Eyes croons out the line about "the final curtain."

"Come now, Father," I hear you protest. "First, you are a pessimist about progress and the advance of science. Now will you attack individualism? We *like* individualism. We admire our pioneers and explorers. Isn't it a good thing to stand out from the herd of lemmings? We admire our inventors and entrepreneurs and are proud of our independent spirit, our 'don't tread on me' attitude, and our 'can do' ethic of hard work and self-reliance. How can you be against individualism?"

Hold your horses. I'm not against any of that, but I am opposed to the sort of individualism that is the personal expression of the relativism I outlined in the previous chapter. The eleventh head of the Hydra, individualism, is not the entrepreneurial, independent spirit we so admire. It is a proud spirit that stands alone, independent of any authority, any truth, any reality outside its own self-referencing bubble. I'm referring to the individualism that is the lie that there is nothing other than me, myself, and I. The roots of modern individualism lie in the thought of the sixteenth-century French writer Michel de Montaigne. Benjamin and Jenna Storey have explained how Montaigne broke away from any standard set by philosophy, faith, or society simply to be "himself."[29] His hugely influential book of essays established a fresh perspective on the human person—a perspective that was self-referential and centered on one's own intrinsic integrity and honesty. Writing in the wake of the Protestant revolution, Montaigne is the great-grandaddy of modern individualism.

To define the term more specifically, instead of individualism, Carl Trueman uses the term "expressive individualism" and

---

[29] Benjamin Storey and Jenna Silber Storey, *Why We Are Restless: On the Modern Quest for Contentment* (Princeton: Princeton University Press, 2021), chap. 1.

explains how modern man has reimagined himself as the center of his own universe.

The Loneliness of Relativism

The sort of individualism I am opposing is connected with all the other fanged heads we have been considering.

If there is no spiritual realm, and therefore no source of truth outside one's physical perceptions, then every man is an island after all. Each person is adrift in his own lifejacket—shipwrecked and bobbing on the sea in the darkness of the night.

In a historic sermon just before his election as Pope Benedict XVI, Joseph Ratzinger spoke about modern man being tossed about. He said:

> Today, having a clear faith based on the creed of the Church is often labeled as fundamentalism. Whereas relativism, that is, letting oneself be "tossed here and there, carried about by every wind of doctrine", seems the only attitude that can cope with modern times. We are building a dictatorship of relativism that does not recognize anything as definitive and whose ultimate goal consists solely of one's ego and desires.[30]

Materialism (which is atheism disguised) demands relativism, which admits there is no external source of truth, and without truth and without God, the individual person is alone in the dark. Yes, there is human love and relationships, but without a greater power and greater truth that transcends our mortal lives, each individual is ultimately alone.

---

[30] Homily at the Mass Pro Eligendo Romano Pontifice, Vatican basilica, April 18, 2005, quoted in Sarah, *God or Nothing*, 180–181.

In the midst of this swirling sea of lies, each individual must find his own way. With no source of authority other than himself, he must wade through the vast amount of information with which he is deluged and try to make sense of the world. Referring to the philosopher Charles Taylor, Carl Trueman explains how, over the last three hundred years, Western man has experienced a shift from perceiving the world as an ordered, meaningful place (into which he must learn to fit harmoniously) to perceiving the world as a random environment onto which he must try to impose some sort of meaning or purpose.[31]

The people of the lie tell us that this self-determination is the passport to happiness and total freedom. In fact, as we shall see, putting oneself in the center of the universe leads not to freedom but to slavery. How does this happen?

Power, Pride, and Prejudice

First, we have to ask, "What drives the individual forward in life? What is the energy and motive force?" Freud said it was sex, Jung thought it was the unconscious, but once again Nietzsche nailed it. He said it was "the will to power." At the root of man's drive for independence is the lust for power. We long to sing with Frank, "I did it my way."

The will to power comes automatically with the gift of choice. In making a choice, I decide that one thing is better than another, and if one thing is better than another, then that thing I chose registers in my mind as something "good." That other thing (which I did not choose) must therefore be less good. As

---

[31] Carl R. Trueman, *The Rise and Triumph of the Modern Self: Cultural Amnesia, Expressive Individualism, and the Road to Sexual Revolution* (Wheaton, IL: Crossway, 2020), 39ff.

a result, the seed of the knowledge of good and evil is planted in my mind.

By making a choice, I have the knowledge of good and evil, and with that, I realize that I can use this power to make further choices. The newfound power immediately creates pride. What is pride? Pride is the basic assumption and rock-solid, bottom-line conviction that, without any doubt, I am right.

Why am I right? I am right because I made that choice, and it must have been the *right* choice — otherwise I would not have chosen it. Pride is built on a circular bit of reasoning that is automatically assumed and therefore unshakable. The conviction that I am right is unshakable because I am blind to it. It is such a fundamental, rock-solid assumption that it simply cannot be wrong. My being right cannot be questioned because the question simply never arises.

This is the monumental flaw of the individual ego. This is the fundamental state of each individual, and this pride — the unshakable assumption that one is right — is at the heart of the kind of expressive individualism to which I am referring.

Furthermore, given the assumptions of materialism (that there is no external authority or source of truth), how can one ever have this false assumption challenged? One cannot. It is the default setting. It is the way each one of us is wired. We are right. Each of us is the king of the universe. The cosmos revolves around us. We'll do it our way. We are almighty.

Unfortunately, the cosmos doesn't have room for more than one Almighty God. It just so happens that there are several billion other individuals, all with their own egos, their own will to power, their own needs and desires, and unfortunately those different egos tend to bump into one another from time to time. So, out of the will to power comes pride — the unshakable conviction that

I am right—and from that pride comes prejudice: the complete and total conviction that *you* are wrong.

If you chose differently from me, then it is obvious that you are wrong, and if my choice was right, it must also have been good. Therefore, your choice (which was wrong) is clearly not only wrong, but bad. What do good people do? They get rid of bad stuff, and if the other people are bad because they chose wrongly, then to get rid of the bad we have to get rid of them, correct? Therefore, if you are wrong and bad and I am right and good, I need to get rid of you. That is why the second story in the book of Genesis tells us how Cain killed his brother Abel.

Reading this, you may well say, "But I'm not like that!" Really? Then you have proven my point that we are blind to the evil interplay of power, pride, and prejudice. Trust me. We are all like that, but we have devised many devious ways to mask our pride and disguise our prejudice and our will to power. In fact, most of our lives are spent denying, deflecting, and dismissing this dark root of the ego, and one of the ways we turn away from the darkness within is in our relationships with others.

Resentment, Rivalry, and Revenge

Each of us, without an external authority or source of truth to correct our egos, will assert our power. Now, of course, it only takes a moment to realize that this simply won't do. We soon learn that we are not Almighty God. There are checks to our power. There are other people more powerful than we are. There are pleasures we can't afford and duties we must perform. There are rules that check our power, and so our ego is restrained, and out of that restraint grows resentment.

This resentment is not simply the regret over Jimmy's getting a bigger piece of pie or Sally's winning the race we wanted to win. The resentment to which I am referring is a deep bitterness over the frustration of our will to power. It may come about as the result of some real wound, or it may be an imagined insult or injury to our ego. It doesn't really matter. What matters is that we nurture the resentment.

We feed it until it turns into a resentment loop that plays over and over again in our minds and hearts. We remember the insult and the injury and lick our wounds. The philosopher Max Scheler observes that we then indulge in four lies.[32] First, we focus our resentment on another person. Next, we generalize the resentment. Our animosity is now aimed not just at one person but at a group of people. It is not that woman who hurt me but *all* women. It is not that white man but *all* white men. It is not my father but *all* fathers.

Next, after brooding over our resentment long enough, we flip the resentment and make it something good in our eyes. We turn our bitterness into our red badge of courage. Because we have suffered, we imagine ourselves the victims, and if victims, then martyrs, and if martyrs, then heroes, and if heroes, thus we come to perceive ourselves as good.

Once this happens, the cycle of self-righteousness is water-tight. Nothing can penetrate the hardened shell around the self-righteous victim. He will not only be better than everyone else; he will use his victimhood to bully everyone else.

The Disintegration of Individualism

Human beings were not designed to be minuscule gods and goddesses. We receive our identity not from ourselves but in relationship with others. "Our sense of selfhood, of who we are, is both

---

[32] Max Scheler, *Ressentiment* (Milwaukee: Marquette University Press, 2007).

intuitive and deeply intertwined with the expectations—ethical and otherwise, of the society in which we are placed. The desire to be recognized, to be accepted, to belong is a deep and perennial human need and no individual sets the terms of that recognition or belonging all by himself."[33]

Consequently, expressive individualism destroys itself in four ways. First, the individualist may turn into a narcissistic psychopath and impose his will on others. Second, he may self-dramatize and wallow in his individualism, resentment, and bitterness as an arrogant lonely dreamer. Third, he may follow his individualism to its logical end into escapist addiction and suicide. Fourth, he may find his identity and acceptance by joining a group of others—a tribe of "individualists" like himself who are just like one another (and therefore not individualists).

The depressed, suicidal, or narcissistic psychopaths we will leave to their own destruction. The individual who joins the tribe is of most interest because it is the most common manifestation in history and in our society today, and this is the twelfth head of the Hydra: tribalism.

This is the ultimate irony of individualism: that those who make the greatest attempt to be individualistic end up being the most conformist. Without any external source of authority, the individualist either ends up completely isolated or he joins a tribe.

In our relativistic society, in which we are increasingly mobile and rootless, in which families are broken by divorce and infidelity, in which education is fragmentary and relativistic, in which employment is temporary and shifting, individuals are increasingly isolated. In a society where there are no agreed values, no agreed philosophy or religion, and no agreed standards,

[33] Trueman, *The Rise and Triumph*, 70.

the individual is adrift and alone. The attraction, therefore, to joining a tribe of some sort is overwhelmingly magnetic.

The tribe may be a group of radical activists rioting in the streets, or it may be a snug little religious group. The tribe may be a sect, a professional club, a union, a political party, a church, or a country club. Within that tribe, the individualist will feel secure and may even think he has joined with a group of like-minded people who are just as individualistic as he is, but this would be a delusion. Instead of developing as a true individual, the person adopts the characteristics of the tribe and becomes a drone — just the opposite of a unique individual.

The distorted dynamic of the group sucks the individual in, and he becomes part of a larger movement that has two destructive characteristics: brainwashing and blame. To increase loyalty to the tribe, propaganda and brainwashing take place, and to enforce groupthink, thought police are empowered. When the tribal behaviors get to this point, free speech does not have to be abolished by force. The tribal members themselves will not allow free speech.

Along with the brainwashing goes blame. The individuals in the tribe — enslaved by pride — cannot be wrong. Their ideology cannot be wrong. Therefore, if there are problems, someone else is always to blame. It may be another tribe, or it may be someone from within the tribe who is blamed for the problems. When the blame and the brainwashing go together, the individuals begin to behave as a group. Individual will and choice evaporate. The mob mentality takes over, and the individual is obliterated.

Tribalistic Catholics

Do not imagine that this sick dynamic operates only in secular circles; this disease has certainly also infected the Church. With the lack of clear authority that comes with the pastoral, dogma-free church, Catholics have become increasingly tribalistic.

Individual parishes follow the personality and opinions of their priests. Laypeople with websites, blogs, and YouTube channels gather to themselves huge followings of uncertain and disenchanted Catholic individuals. Radical traditionalist sects such as the Society of Saint Pius X spring up. Progressive priests, bishops, and religious superiors drive forward their own version of Catholicism. Nationalist and ethnic groups such as the Polish National Catholic Church forge their own cultural forms of the Faith, and within all of them, the same negative tribalistic patterns of behavior can occur.

Thus, individualism turns in on and devours itself. The worst part of this terrible dynamic is that unique individuals become obliterated.

In *The Abolition of Man*, C. S. Lewis wrote a harsh critique of relativism and showed how the group dynamic that destroys the individual also abolishes humanity itself. The individual is swept up and enslaved by demonic powers; and the most frightening thing of all is that each victim will have yielded his individual self willingly.

7

Puppy Dogs and Women Priests

Sentimentalism and Romanticism

I was a minister in the Church of England in the late 1980s, when the entire denomination was embroiled in a debate about women's ordination. Much was at stake. Strong arguments were put forward from both sides, and the debates became heated. Very often the discussion was reduced to one-sided speeches like this:

> My friend Sandra is a deacon. She has received the same theological training as the priests. She is a good preacher and teacher. She is a compassionate person who loves God and loves her neighbor. I know Sandra as a prayerful, mature, and humble person. She has three beautiful children and a loving husband. You would love to see her walking in the countryside with Derek and their pair of Labradors, Poppy and George. Is it fair to deny Sandra ordination to the priesthood when she has felt in the depth of her heart that she, too, is called by God to be a priest?

The appeal in this speech is not to theology or Scripture. It is not to reason, Church tradition, the writings of the apostolic

Fathers, canon law, or the beliefs of Anglicanism's older sisters, the Catholic and Orthodox churches.

The appeal is pure sentimentality. It is an appeal to the emotions. We are expected to admire Sandra for her wonderful qualities. Our hearts are warmed by her personal integrity, her deep faith, her status as wife and mother, and her fondness for her two lovable Labradors.

Then the propagandists plunged in the emotional blackmail dagger: "How can you be so cruel and heartless to deny Sandra what she knows God wants her to do?"

Sentimentalism is the thirteenth head of the Hydra that needs to be cut off and cauterized. There is nothing wrong with emotion as such, but sentimentalism is the system of decision-making or taking an action based *only* on one's emotions.

The philosopher Alasdair MacIntyre defines sentimentalism as "the doctrine that all evaluative judgments and more specifically all moral judgments are *nothing but* expressions of preference, expressions of attitude or feeling, insofar as they are moral or evaluative in character."[34]

Remember that the heads of the Hydra are all interwoven, and so sentimentalism is often combined with utilitarianism and pragmatism, with deadly results: "I'm afraid your mother is nearing the end of her life" says the kindly doctor. "I know you do not wish her to be in pain any longer. She's a lovely person, but there really is not much more we can do for her. I'm going to leave this medicine here on her bedside table. I'm not allowed to administer it, but if you want her to be relieved of pain, just

---

[34] Alastair MacIntyre, *After Virtue: A Study in Moral Theory* (London: Bloomsbury, 2013), 13, quoted in Trueman, *The Rise and Triumph*, 85.

add it to her cup of tea before bed, and she will drift off to sleep. She will be at peace, and everyone will feel much better."

Wherever you turn, sentimentalism rules. Arguments are made, goods are sold, relationships are undertaken and broken, decisions are taken based only on emotion. We think toleration, a positive attitude, and being nice are the ruling emotions, but tenderness is not the only powerful emotion. There are other emotions lurking in the shadows. Rage, resentment, fear, and hatred are feelings too. They are the shadow side of sentimentalism.

All Heart, No Head

It is easy to write sentimentalism off as so much inconsequential fluff, but the roots of sentimentalism go deep into the other errors we have already explored. Like the other heads of the Hydra, sentimentalism springs from the materialistic atheism that lies at the heart of the beast. If there is no Heaven or Hell, no God as a source of truth, then we are left on our own. In the face of relativism and with no source of truth, some people resort to their own opinions, intellectual theories, and ideologies. Others turn not to the head, but to the heart.

The deeper philosophy and cultural movement behind sentimentalism is the fourteenth head of the Hydra—romanticism. This cultural movement began in the late eighteenth century and blossomed in the nineteenth. The poetry, novels, paintings, and music of romanticism gush with powerful emotions. This is the period of some of the best-loved and most emotionally powerful works of art: the stirring music of Beethoven and Brahms, the operas of Verdi and Puccini, the paintings of the pre-Raphaelites and the Impressionists, the emotional and evocative poetry of Wordsworth, Shelley, Keats, and Coleridge. This is also the period of the frightening gothic stories of Dr. Frankenstein, Dr.

Jekyll and Mr. Hyde, the horror tales of Edgar Allen Poe, and the sweeping romances of the Brontë sisters.

As we have seen, the Enlightenment thinkers replaced divine revelation with a reliance on human reason. When pure rationalism proved to be abstract, sterile, and uninspiring, however, mankind, starved for inspiration, truth, and beauty, fell in love with subjective emotion. The rationalist Descartes said, "I think; therefore, I am." The Romantics brushed that aside and said, "I feel; therefore, I am."

The historian of ideas Isaiah Berlin observed that, for over a century, romanticism disrupted Western traditions of rationality and the idea of moral absolutes and agreed values, leading "to something like the melting away of the very notion of objective truth."[35]

Rousseau, the First Sentimentalist

The writer and philosopher Jean-Jacques Rousseau (d. 1778) was born in Geneva, Switzerland—the nexus of Calvinism. Rousseau's mother died soon after he was born. His father was a passionate, weak, immature man who soon abandoned his family.

Rousseau bounced from foster homes to boarding schools before setting out on his own. As a teenager, he converted to Catholicism and fell in with an older woman. His life was a tempestuous adventure of love affairs, philosophical and political debates, battles with religious authorities over his heretical writings, and stormy friendships with other Enlightenment writers and philosophers, such as David Hume, Denis Diderot, and Voltaire.

---

[35] Isaiah Berlin, *The Crooked Timber of Humanity* (Princeton: Princeton University Press, 2013), 60.

I consider Rousseau the first sentimentalist. Why? It can be summed up by an incident in his life retold by historian Joseph T. Stuart. Rousseau was walking along a road when he spotted an ad for an essay competition that read, "Has the progress of the sciences and arts contributed to corrupt or purify morals?" This question enflamed his mind and heart:

> Perhaps humans are naturally good? Perhaps evil proceeds not from the heart of man, but from the constraint and competition of an artificial civilization? Maybe we need to return to our natural simplicity in order to be whole? From the moment he read these words in a magazine, Rousseau wrote, "I beheld another world and became another man." Dazzled by a thousand sparkling lights as crowds of lively ideas thronged his mind, he felt giddy and intoxicated. With difficulty breathing and palpitations of the heart, he threw himself down under a tree and "there passed a half hour in such agitation that on rising I found the whole front of my shirt wet with tears, without having been conscious that I had shed them."[36]

Rousseau was a victim of the Protestant Revolution that took place two hundred years earlier. John Calvin taught the total depravity of man, and in reaction, Rousseau had a highly sentimental experience in which he had a vision of the total goodness of man.

The Catholic Church teaches neither the total depravity and sinfulness of man nor the total goodness of man. Instead, she teaches that God created man in His divine image and said,

---

[36] Joseph T. Stuart, *Rethinking the Enlightenment: Faith in the Age of Reason* (Manchester, NH: Sophia Institute Press, 2020), 21–22.

"That's good!" We are good, but we have fallen. God's image in us is wounded. We need redemption, healing, and restoration.

Rousseau was, in some ways, a great soul, but he was also deeply wounded and flawed. He went on to study and write on botany, philosophy, and political science. His dependence on personal emotion was linked with a sentimental understanding of nature. As he threw himself down under a tree in his life-changing moment of enlightenment, so Rousseau would glorify the solitary, romantic attachment to nature—taking long, lonely walks to commune within himself with the beauties of the natural world.

Rousseau's individualistic, sentimental understanding of the self and the world is very much part of the assumed modern mindset. It is present, first of all, in our denial of Original Sin and our belief that circumstances and external societal influences are the cause of human wrongdoing. It is present in our sentimental attitudes toward animals and nature, and it is expressed through misguided or extreme environmentalism and campaigns for animal rights. It is present in our modern assumption that romantic love excuses everything, and above all, it is present in the ideas that our own emotions are the only test for truth.

Original Goodness

Rousseau died in 1778, but the ideas he planted were hugely influential in the century to follow. Suddenly God's revelation was not the source of truth, nor was man's philosophy the answer. Instead, the surge of inner emotions was the criteria for truth, and it was the artist, not the theologian or the philosopher, who became the high priest and guardian of truth, and this reliance on "the inner light" spread through every aspect of society.

Isaiah Berlin observes the following:

In the realm of ethics, politics, aesthetics it was the authenticity and sincerity of the pursuit of inner goals that mattered; this applied equally to individuals and groups—states, nations, movements. This is most evident in the aesthetics of romanticism, where the notion of eternal models, a Platonic vision of ideal beauty, which the artist seeks to convey, however imperfectly, on canvas or in sound, is replaced by a passionate belief in spiritual freedom, individual creativity. The painter, the poet, the composer do not hold up a mirror to nature ... but create not merely the means but the goals that they pursue; these goals represent the self-expression of the artist's own unique, inner vision, to set aside which in response to the demands of some "external" voice—church, state, public opinion, family friends, arbiters of taste—is an act of betrayal of what alone justifies their existence for those who are in any sense creative.[37]

Rousseau also brought his sentimental subjectivism to bear on political theory. Inspired by his experience on the road to Vincennes, his dominant conviction was the essential goodness of man. "We are not bad," Rousseau would contend. "It is a corrupt society that makes us bad. And who controls that society? It is the establishment: the wealthy, the aristocrats, the Church."

The common man, however, must be good because mankind is good. Therefore, the intentions of the crowd of common men must also be good, and when each individual joins with others, his own goodness is validated and strengthened. When this is

---

[37] Berlin, *The Crooked Timber of Humanity*, 60.

extended to society, the conclusion must be that the will of the majority is also automatically and essentially good.

Puppies and Kittens Spirituality

It is no surprise that sentimentalism swept the Church along with pastoral, dogma-free emphasis in the 1960s. Out went dogma and clear moral teaching. In came felt banners, folk songs, Father Feelgood, Sister Sandals, and sentimental spirituality. The Catholics went along with the mainstream Protestants in embracing a sweet spirituality based on the individual's subjective feelings.

When faced with giving advice on moral questions, pastors sidestepped the clear teaching of the Catholic Church and said their parishioners should always be guided by their conscience. By "their conscience" they did not mean a conscience well formed by truths revealed by God through the Scriptures and the Church. They meant "go with your feelings." This emphasis on the priority of the individual conscience is also the fruit of the romantic movement.

The liturgies, music, architecture, and art all went with the sentimentality of the age. Despite its sweet appearance, sentimentality is always destructive. Following Rousseau's belief, the old hidebound establishment is the enemy of the beautiful, enlightened individual feelings, so all that "old, hidebound, musty, dusty religious stuff" was consigned to the garbage heap, to be replaced with the ephemeral, the ugly, the shallow, and the cheap trinkets of modern sentimental Catholicism.

More disturbing than the sentimental devotions and shallow liturgies is the theological fallout from Rousseau's thought. Universalism is the belief that everyone will be saved in the end. Never mind that this contradicts the clear words of the Lord Jesus. Ralph Martin shows that universalism is the prevailing trend not only in the mainstream Protestant churches but also in the highest levels of the Catholic Church.[38]

Universalism can be summed up with the following sentimental statement: "I can't believe God would be so mean as to send anyone to Hell." Such an inane statement is rooted in Rousseau's belief that all of us are essentially good at heart. Not only does universalism contradict the plain words of Scripture; it also eliminates free will. Are we saying that God is going to force people into Heaven? This sounds like the utilitarian dictator who says, "You *will* be happy!"

Universalism also contradicts common sense, common human decency, and the demand for justice. Does the universalist really believe that a person who plans a kidnapping, then tortures, rapes, and slowly kills little children—all without the slightest bit of regret—should go to Heaven? Come now. This is foolishness, and the fact that universalism has become mainstream shows just how far sentimentalism has eaten away the foundations of the Faith.

This same absurd sentimentality is evident in the naïve assumptions of our society. No matter what horrors have been planned and perpetrated by the majority, we still assume that, because man is good, the plans he makes for society must also be good. We also assume that majority equals morality. The mob may riot and rampage, pillage and rape, but we still believe their revolution is noble, that they are good at heart and their motives are pure. This disastrous assumption fuels the revolution and the rise of tyranny. It does so because all the isms interact with each

---

[38]   See chapter 3 of Ralph Martin, *A Church in Crisis: Pathways Forward* (Steubenville, OH: Emmaus Road, 2020). Martin's thoroughgoing critique of universalism is *Will Many Be Saved?: What Vatican II Actually Teaches and Its Implications for the New Evangelization* (Grand Rapids, MI: William B. Eerdmans, 2012).

other. Sentimentalism is the natural expression of individualism. The individual's emotions rule all. Sentimentalism is linked with utilitarianism because the feeling that the individual is innately good brings about the conclusion that the feelings of the crowd must also be good, and utilitarianism is the belief that happiness for the crowd is good. Sentimentalism, therefore, also feeds progressivism and utopianism: if mankind is essentially good, then he is advancing to ever higher levels of goodness, and the dream of an ideal society produces another wave of wonderful, positive feelings.

Tenderness and Tyranny

When these isms come together, we can see why nationalism, fascism, Nazism, and communism were the results. Because of the flawed assumption of individual and societal goodness, the crowd swallows the utopian lie. With a dream of total group happiness, the masses fall under the sway of a leader who promises a heaven on earth, and they are swept up in a tsunami of emotional political fervor—a fervor that swells and surges and sweeps them up in an ever spiraling whirlwind of emotion.

Finally, because personal emotions are always good and are the ultimate guide to goodness, when the not-so-nice emotions emerge, they too are regarded as good. Resentment is an emotion. Rage is an emotion. Fear is an emotion. When the fear and resentment surge forth in an irrational wave, the people who are filled with rage believe that their rage—and the accompanying violence—is justified.

They have already come to believe that all their emotions are good. They have come to believe their cause is righteous, and if religion is thrown into the mix, in their hearts they know that God is also on their side. Therefore, they revel in the negative emotions of resentment and rage, and this reinforces another emotion that is invincible: self-righteousness.

Once these negative emotions are unleashed, there is no stopping the volcano of violence. This is why Rousseau's sweet ideas about the goodness of human nature eventually ended in the Reign of Terror and Madame Guillotine. As Flannery O'Connor observed, "Tenderness leads to the gas chamber." Sentimentalism — the rule of individualistic emotion — ends by destroying not only the good and beautiful emotions of the individual but also the individual himself.

8

The Weirdness of Barbie and Ken

Eroticism and Freudianism

In 1959, at the American International Toy Fair, the Mattel company launched the Barbie doll. Marketing the doll as a "teen-aged fashion model," Mattel sold more than 350,000 units in the first year alone.

Has it ever struck you how weird the Barbie doll is? Think about it. What is childlike about the Barbie doll? With her pneumatic chest, impossible waist, stork-like legs, and pouting expression, if she is a teenager, her name is Lolita.

Ruth Handler, the creator of the Barbie doll, borrowed the idea from a German doll named Bild Lilli, "a blonde bombshell, a working girl who knew what she wanted and was not above using men to get it." In other words, she was a German Marilyn Monroe.

So we gave our little girls Marilyn Monroe dolls to play with? Before 1959, little girls played with baby dolls, not Barbie dolls. Playtime is practice for adulthood, and when girls played house and tucked their baby dolls into bed, they were preparing for their future roles as wives and mothers. What were they modeling when they played with Barbie? They were modeling models, and not just fashion models but a new kind of American woman—one who was not primarily a wife and mother but a busty clothes horse who reveled in a full closet, a dream home, a flashy sports car, and Ken.

And who or what is Ken? The third *Toy Story* film features a hilarious send-up of Barbie and Ken. Barbie is a ditzy blonde who gets all excited when she meets Ken, who is portrayed as a campy gay man. Like most satire, it bites because it's true. If Barbie was "a blonde bombshell, a working girl who knew what she wanted and was not above using men to get it," Ken was not a husband and father. He was the quintessential, effeminate, modern man: well-quaffed and suntanned, gossiping with the girls and fussing over his outfits.

At the same time in the 1950s, the eugenicist Margaret Sanger raised money for the development of the contraceptive pill, which was legalized in 1960—the year after Barbie made her debut. As the sexual act was separated from procreation, women were separated from motherhood, and little girls were given a doll that helped them think of themselves as sex objects instead of mothers. I don't for a moment imagine that any of this was intentional. Nevertheless, Barbie and Ken reflected the shift in sexual roles and behaviors that was taking place in the wider society during the 1950s, '60s, and '70s.

Marilyn, Not Mother

I know you will think I am the ultimate spoilsport. First, I slash Disneyworld, now Barbie. "What American icon is next for the knife?" you may ask, "McDonald's? Apple pie? Baseball? The Statue of Liberty? Tom Hanks?"

I'm sorry, but the critique of Barbie as the Marilyn Monroe doll leads to a bigger issue. The shift was simple. It was Marilyn Monroe instead of mother. The sex goddess of the silver screen became the one the men adored and the women had to emulate.

Marilyn's curvaceous figure and bouncy body was not for marriage and childbearing. It was for playtime. *Playboy* was also launched in the 1950s, and the magazine's sudden success was fueled by its famous Marilyn Monroe nude centerfold.

The change in sexual beliefs and behaviors in the second half of the twentieth century was the most revolutionary of all the revolutions in the five hundred years that had gone before. We now live in a society in which the general rule about sex is that there are no rules about sex. The idea that unrestrained sexual pleasure is the greatest good is the fifteenth head of the Hydra—the one called eroticism. "With sexual pleasure as the one imperious good, all values are inverted. God ... standing as an obstacle to abortion and sexual pleasure, becomes bad."[39]

This cultural earthquake was facilitated by three factors. The first was the invention of cheap, effective, artificial birth control. For the first time in history, human beings could turn off the baby machine. The invention of artificial contraception is more shattering than any other invention in human history—the taming of fire, the invention of the wheel, moveable type, electricity, the microprocessor, or any other invention you might name. Its consequences for the human race have been seismic, and its shockwaves are reverberating in ways we are still struggling to understand.

Beautiful Urges

The second factor was philosophical, and it is linked with the isms we have already considered. This is the treatment of sex as the sublime fulfillment of personal freedom. This romantic notion

---

[39] George Gilder, foreword to Michael D. Aeschliman, *The Restitution of Man: C. S. Lewis and the Case Against Scientism* (Grand Rapids, MI: William B. Eerdmans, 1998), 8.

can be traced back to Jean-Jacques Rousseau. He was not only famous for his individualistic and sentimental notions. He acted on his beliefs. In fact, one could well ask which came first: his infidelity and immorality or his theories justifying his behavior.

Rousseau's first lover was an older woman with whom he was involved in a *ménage à trois*. He had many affairs, and his long-term mistress, Therese, bore him four or five children, all of whom he packed off to an orphanage, after convincing his paramour that she should give up her children for the sake of "her honor."

Rousseau's novel *Julie: The New Helen*, in which his hero-ine — a married woman — falls in love with another man, swept the imagination of Europe. Readers wept in ecstasy as they read it. The publishers could not keep up with demand, and Rous-seau's celebrity status went through the stratosphere. The novel was revolutionary and set a new standard not only for romantic literature, but for a passionate defense of individual feelings, erotic infatuation, and sexual liberation.

Regarding Rousseau's novel, Joseph T. Stuart comments, "A philosophical theory pervades it. Autonomy and authenticity, not rational principles, should serve as the foundation of moral deci-sions. One should conform to society only if such conformity agrees with the deepest feelings that make up one's core identity.... In an age when adultery and casual sex were as common as marrying for status rather than for love, readers found this new morality revo-lutionary." Rousseau's creed was "True love is natural and involves intense romantic and well-intentioned feelings. What distorts this love are social prejudices that smother the human heart."[40]

---

[40] Claudia Durst Johnson and Vernon Johnson, *The Social Impact of the Novel: A Reference Guide* (Westport: Greenwood, 2002), 129–130, quoted in Stuart, *Rethinking the Enlightenment*, 33.

If the rules are merely derived from society, as Rousseau argued, then they restrict man's essential goodness. If every individual is essentially good, then his natural urges must also be good. Therefore, the sexual urges that are part of the beautiful romantic feelings must be not only legitimate but sublime and even divine, and they should not be stifled.

This is why, in modern society, the restraints expected from Christian moralists simply do not compute. Following the materialists and Darwinists, the majority in our society perceive the world as a random, morality-free environment. They are with Rousseau. They believe that they and their urges are essentially good and that restrictions on sexual behavior are no more than the imposition of out-of-date and absurd rules and regulations by a repressive religion and society. Their only creed is "If it feels good, do it." Furthermore, they believe they are not only right to flout the rules; they are also being "true to themselves" and by "expressing their sexuality" are actually doing something good.

Sex and Catholics

Has this philosophy infected the Church like all the others? Of course it has.

The biggest conflict in the Church in modern America has been not only the widespread disregard for the Church's ban on artificial contraceptives but also the mainstream Christian churches' "don't ask, don't tell" approach to sexual discipline and their support for abortion (with a good number of Catholics also joining that campaign).

Christians of all traditions have pretty much gone along with the sexual revolution. The statistics for Christian indulgence in premarital sex, divorce, remarriage, and acceptance of same-sex "marriage" pretty much run parallel with the opinions and actions of the non-Christian population.[41]

In the face of the sexual revolution, Christian teaching on sexual morality was seen as a seemingly absurd list of do's and don'ts enforced by scare tactics that suddenly didn't apply. Our grandfathers would have warned our fathers not to "do it" because they might "get a girl into trouble" — or, if our fathers went with bad women, they would get a horrible, incurable disease. When our dads repeated the age-old warnings, we said, "Don't worry. That was then. This is now. She's on the Pill, and we have antibiotics."

Christian moralists suddenly found their book of tricks was obsolete. Why shouldn't the teens enjoy themselves? "Nobody is getting hurt," they argued. "What's the big deal?"

The Science of Sex

This pragmatic approach reminds us that one of the effects of scientism is to remove any metaphysical meaning from the physical world. The material world is merely something to be studied, dissected, and analyzed. Consequently, sex, like every other aspect of the material world, becomes a subject for analysis.

The Romantics glamorized and dramatized the individual's erotic longings, but the other reaction was the supposedly objective study of sexuality. The atheist psychoanalyst Sigmund Freud (d. 1939) saw the desire for sexual pleasure as the dominant force in the human personality. He followed Rousseau, whom he admired, by saying that religion and society frustrated sexual urges. Rousseau thought sexual urges were sublime and beautiful. Freud thought they were more basic. They were simply the

---

[41] Douthat, *Bad Religion*, 71–72.

animalistic instinct to reproduce and experience sexual pleasure, and repressing them was unhealthy.

One generation after Freud, the sex researcher Alfred Kinsey (d. 1956) founded the science of "sexology." His highly controversial reports also treated sex as no more than a subject to be studied scientifically. The effect of Kinsey and Freud on modern culture has been enormous. The twentieth century has been called "the century of Freud,"[42] and Freudianism is the sixteenth head of the Hydra.

Freudianism can be defined as the understanding of sex as mere instinct. According to Freudian theory, repression of the sexual urge causes neuroses, guilt, and distortions of all kinds. Because the restrictions on sexual behavior were artificial and destructive, they should be abandoned. Attempting to treat sex "scientifically," Freudianism separates the sexual act from any moral restraints and any sense of personal responsibility. Freudianism says, "Sex is a fact of life. It's no big deal. Get over it."

The Downward Spiral of Eroticism

The cheerful hedonist will agree, "Come now. You're treating this all much too seriously. Wanting sex is no different from wanting a hamburger. Sex is like tennis. It's fun if you have a good partner. That's why it's called *Playboy*. We're just boys playing around! It's harmless pleasure."

But sex is not just a game. It is our physical connection with the generation of life itself, and to put physical pleasure as the sole purpose of sex is to head into a disastrous downward spiral.

---

[42] Armand M. Nicholi Jr., *The Question of God: C. S. Lewis and Sigmund Freud Debate God, Sex, Love and the Meaning of Life* (New York: Free Press, 2002), 2.

Whenever a secondary good is placed first in one's priorities, the secondary good will eventually be destroyed.[43] In the chapter on individualism, we saw how a complete devotion to individualism destroys the individual. Likewise, sentimentalism destroys authentic good emotions as they are overwhelmed by the emotions of anger, rage, and resentment. In a similar way, when sex is made the primary good, sex eventually implodes.

Those who put sexual pleasure as the first priority in life will be discontented because their appetites are not being met. They search for other partners and ever more exciting experiences. The more a desire is yielded to, the more debauched such people become. Pornography addicts admit that they began with pictures of normal sex acts but were drawn to increasingly depraved images and actions.

The same thing happened in the wake of romanticism in the nineteenth century. Most of the famous artists, poets, and musicians of the romantic movement lived according to Rousseau's creed. They gave free rein to their passions and lived openly dissolute lives. Many were locked in drug addiction and ended in suicide and the madness brought on by venereal disease.

By the late nineteenth century, the romantic movement had degenerated into the decadent movement. This cultural trend was characterized by self-disgust, sickness at the world, total cynicism, delight in perversion, and employment of crude, macabre, and nihilistic humor. The decadent movement was totally opposed to nature — both in its biological sense and in anything that was normal.

The decadent artists rejected any idea of objective truth and despised even the suggestion that a search for truth was possible.

[43] Aeschliman, *The Restitution of Man*, 25.

Wallowing in nihilism, they believed only in the sensual experience of the moment. They lived for luxury and pleasure and delighted in the exotic, the strange, and the perverse. Drugs and alcohol were used to alter consciousness and indulge in depraved behaviors. Homosexuality and transsexualism became fashionable. A fascination with horror—the bizarre, the shocking, the violent, and the gory—and an obsession with the occult shadowed those who had drifted down into the swamp of Lerna.

This is not just a wholesome romp and healthy sex. This is distorted and degraded humanity, and it is leading to the destruction of sex and human reproduction. The number of young men and women marrying and having children is plummeting. Experts project that the declining birth rate across the globe will usher in a "demographic winter." There is a disturbing rise in young men choosing not to seek a sexual partner at all, and psychologists link this to the rise in pornography. Put bluntly, a real girl who becomes a wife is not worth the trouble compared with the Barbie dolls of porn combined with self-pleasure.

We have become sex sick, and the sickness is a weird distortion of what sex is and what it is for. We see evidence of this distortion all about us. Extreme feminism, homosexualism, transgenderism, pornography and masturbation, prostitution, abortion, artificial contraception, human trafficking, sexual abuse of children, incest, adultery, fornication, fetishism, sadomasochism—these sins are forbidden because they abuse and distort the parts of our bodies that make us men and women and therefore human beings.

Adam and Eve Revisited

This sickness is a sign that we are deeply confused about sex, and if we are confused about our sexuality, then we are confused about who we are, and about humanity itself. This is because sex is at the core of our identity as individuals and as human beings.

When I am preparing couples for marriage, I ask them a simple question: "What is a man? What is a woman?"

Most of the potential brides and grooms look a bit embarrassed, thinking it might be a trick question. Then they stammer out some answers based in social determinants. "A man is a provider" or "A woman is a carer."

I answer, "No. Those are things some men do and some women do. Think again. What is it that makes a man a man and a woman a woman?"

Looking even more embarrassed, they will finally say, "A man has a penis and testicles. The woman has breasts and a womb."

"And what are those organs for?" I ask.

Now they're getting it. "To reproduce."

"Correct. So a man has certain physical characteristics which define him as a father or a potential father. A woman has other physical characteristics that define her as a mother or a potential mother.

That is what a man *is*. That is what a woman *is*. A man is a father or a potential father. A woman is a mother or a potential mother. This is why Adam and Eve were naked in the garden—so they could get the fundamental facts about who they were and why they were created. That's why the first commandment God gave them was "Be fruitful and multiply." In other words, "Make love and make babies."

The fact that I need to have this conversation with young couples, and the fact that, through this dialogue, you can see a moment of enlightenment taking place, is an indication of how profound and widespread the confusion about sexuality really is in our society.

Are you bewildered by the rise of feminism, homosexualism, transgenderism, people being "non-binary," and the suggestion that there are umpteen genders? The reason is simple: we have forgotten that a man is a father or a potential father and a woman is a mother or a potential mother. We've forgotten those simple facts because we have refused to acknowledge what the reproductive and nurturing organs are for, and we refuse to acknowledge what those physical features are for because we have been abusing them for our own pleasure.

If we have forgotten what a man is and what a woman is, we have also forgotten what a human being is, because a human being is either a man or a woman. This confusion is not an insignificant social problem or a personal hang-up. It is a profound crisis for the whole human race.

This chapter has been a grim summary of where the sixteen heads of the Hydra have brought us. In the next section, we will see, in dramatic form, what the future of this sad new world looks like.

The first section of isms dealt with the temptations of the world. The second section explained the temptations of the flesh. In this third section, we will use a dramatic dialogue to explore the horrible consequences of these philosophies. It will illustrate how the sixteen isms are interlocked into one complete and complex temptation.

It is no coincidence that the characters I use to illustrate my point come from a horror story.

I warn you that you will find some of the content in this dialogue disturbing. I do not apologize — because the facts themselves are disturbing and should make all of us wake up to the realities all around us.

The Devil

In the following chapter, the sixteen isms are illustrated and brought to life through a conversation with the devil.

9

Dialogue with the Devil

The scene is a scholar's study in mid-sixteenth-century Germany. It is three o'clock in the morning.

The darkness in the high-ceilinged room is punctuated with candle-light. Bookshelves line the walls. Books, maps, and manuscripts are stacked everywhere. The tables are crowded with paper and pens, tools, an astrolabe, potted plants, scales, telescopes, and bottles of potions, biological specimens, and all the various paraphernalia for scientific experiments.

A middle-aged man is slumped in an old leather chair. Dr. Faustus has been up all night agonizing over a philosophical problem: Does man have a soul?

There is a knock on the door.

DR. FAUST. Who is it? Who is calling at this hour?

MEPHISTOPHELES. I require lodging. Is there room at the inn?

FAUST. This is not an inn.

The door opens, and a well-dressed gentleman enters. He removes his hat and cloak and bows in greeting.

MEPHISTOPHELES. You will forgive me, I hope? The reference to an inn was a literary allusion. You know. The stranger of Bethlehem?

FAUST. Yes. Yes. What do you want?

M. As I said, I am looking for lodging. Alas. The foxes have holes and the birds of the air have nests, but the Son of Man has nowhere to lay his head.

F. Another literary allusion. The Gospel of Matthew.

M., *taking off his gloves and making to sit down.* Chapter eight, verse twenty. May I?

F. I suppose so. Yes. Be seated. In fact, I welcome some company and conversation. The night is long.

M. And you cannot sleep. I know the feeling well.

F. Can I get you a drink of some sort?

M. Wine, I think. Red wine, if you please. I prefer it to be warmed—body temperature. I see you are a scholar. Perhaps you were unable to sleep because you were pondering some great problem? An enigma? A puzzle? A conundrum? A great mystery?

F., *placing a glass and bottle of wine on the table.* That is my life. I am a professor of philosophy.

M. Indeed, but from what I can see, you are more than that. All this evidence of scientific experimentation. You must be a man of great learning. Not just a philosopher, but an alchemist, perhaps?

F. Yes, but not an alchemist in the crude sense.

M. I know what you mean. Those rather common, grubby little men who spend their time trying to turn lead into gold.

F. They understand so little. They think alchemy is merely a way to get rich. True alchemy is the search not simply for gold but for the way to understand the mysterious workings of the material world.

M. Yes, yes. Indeed. I couldn't agree more. However . . . a certain amount of gold doesn't go amiss, I think? One cannot live on bread alone. The laborer is worth of his hire, is he not? While you are searching for higher things, I'm sure you wouldn't refuse a bag of gold if that were part of the bargain?

F. Of course not, but the true alchemist searches for the elixir of life—the key to immortality.

M., *laughs*. How noble you are, sir! The search for eternal life! Surely that is the territory of the priests and monks, is it not? Didn't their master say, "I am the resurrection and the life?" If you are searching for eternal life—whatever that may be—surely you are in the wrong profession?

F. Do you think I have not considered that? I have looked into their claims and found them wanting. Their Heaven is no more than a bribe for frightened souls and their Hell a threat of torture. I have found no evidence for Heaven or Hell.

M. A man after my own heart! I, too, have pondered these questions and come to the same conclusions. There is no Heaven or Hell, and I expect we also agree about the so-called angels and demons?

F. The stuff of children's stories, dreams, and nightmares. This is reality: the knowledge in these books. The discoveries I have made with these instruments, this experimentation. This world is reality.

M. Indeed. What a magnificent mind you have! To have learned so much and gained so much wisdom. But is not this life of yours a lonely existence? May I suggest that there are other realities here in this world that you have yet to discover?

F. Perhaps. I'm intrigued. What would they be?

M. My friend. May I call you friend? Perhaps I may even call you brother? The knowledge you have gained from these books and your experimentation has served you well, but there is also the knowledge of experience. I am talking about the greatest mystery of all — the mystery of love.

F. You mean a woman? I cannot be bothered with a nagging wife and a house full of brawling brats.

M., *shudders*. Of course. My word! Indeed. Indeed! I wasn't referring to anything so common and low as some corpulent wench with a bald and toothless brat sucking her teat — like some disgusting piglet. I was referring to something far more noble and refined. A beautiful young woman — a soul mate is what you need.

F. How so?

M. For a man like you, a beautiful young woman is an inspiration, a joy, and a delight. She opens for you the regions of the heart, not just the mind. She is the *anima* — the feminine genius — and your love for her will help you to discover new regions of knowledge and wisdom. Surely you knew that in the ancient world wisdom was always personified as woman — and who was the first divine beauty who ate of the tree of knowledge but the delectable Eva?

F. I don't know how to begin. I've never been with a woman. Would I ... You know ...

M. Would you enjoy her carnal delights? But of course! Would you say you had enjoyed this wine if the bottle remained in your cellar? No! You open it. You taste it, and so you come to know the wine. It is the same with a woman. You come to know her wisdom by being one with her. The sublime ecstasy of true knowledge!

F. This is true knowledge? I had never seen it that way before. To me, the mind and the search for wisdom was the higher way. The base physical pleasures seemed to me vulgar — low and sordid.

M. I understand, but if I may say so, that is an immature viewpoint. I am not talking simply about crude pleasure. That may be found with the coarse hoydens of the demimonde. I am talking about a great *affaire de coeur* — an affair not just of the body but of the heart. To yield to those passions of the heart can open the way to knowledge just as much as, or more than, pursuing the passions of the head alone! The knowledge that is revealed in the greatest of physical delights is the true knowledge of oneself. This is the paradox, is it not — that there in the rummaging and fumblings below the waist we descend to the lower regions not only of the body but also of who we really are. We discover the beast, and, in that, do we not also discover the beauty? Only by descending into the dark caverns of desire can we find the eternal light of who we really are.

F. But what if there is progeny?

M. Offspring? It is not a problem. We have always had ways to do away with such trifles. You can leave that to me. There are pragmatic solutions.

F. And you will arrange this for me? You can do this?

M. It is not quite so simple as that. I do not give you the gold or the woman you desire, but I can give you the knowledge you still lack. Once you have unlimited knowledge, the gold and the pleasure will follow as night follows day.

F. Certainly what you say is true. I have already experienced this. Knowledge is power. With enough knowledge, one can do anything.

M. Yes, yes! With knowledge, all things are possible! Let me give you an example. What problem were you pondering when I knocked on the door? You were wrestling with the question of whether man has an immortal soul, were you not?

F. How did you know that?

M. I know everything. That is why I can promise you ultimate knowledge. If you follow me, I will lead you into all truth. This question, for example—does man have an immortal soul? The answer is yes and no.

F. Tell me more.

M. Man does not have an immortal soul. You know this from your scientific discoveries. Have you found any evidence for this "soul"?

F. I have not.

M. Just so. For man to have an immortal soul, he would have to have had such a thing given to him by some greater immortal being. I believe you have also come to the conclusion that such an immortal being outside the created order is a figment of a frightened child's imagination. Is that not so?

F. It is so, but I have not published my beliefs.

M. That is understandable. However, to return to our original question: Does man have an immortal soul? The answer is: No, he does not. But yes—he may.

F. You mean he may develop an immortal soul?

M. Yes! Man is developing. He is evolving into an ever greater and greater being. This is the true meaning of history! Rising from the apes, he is forever gaining new knowledge and experience. The time will come when he reaches what one of our children called "the omega point," when he will move on to the next stage and blossom into his full humanity. He will gain immortality, and with it, an immortal soul.

F. This is truly intriguing. It is the answer to my question. After all these years, I can see it. It is through complete knowledge that we will become immortal.

M. Yes. Knowledge of this material realm. No longer will humanity need the idea of God because they will become gods. They will emerge as the Übermensch — the supermen. They will be the immortals. Then history will be their story.

F. The pioneers.

M. Truly. Truly! The pioneers. Yes! An apt phrase. A few of us have already trod that lonely path. A few of the enlightened ones are already here looking for disciples, and this is what brought me to your door on this dark night. If you wish to follow in my footsteps, the knowledge I give you will bring you untold wealth. The gold will simply flow to you. You will also experience the ecstasy and joy of knowing a woman and gaining that eternal knowledge of your true self. Most of all, you will be a forerunner of the new age. This age of mankind will be total and complete. It will take another five hundred years, but I can give you a glimpse of this brave, new world.

F. How will you do this?

M. Come. Let us look into this telescope. You use it to study the stars, do you not?

F. I do.

M. Let us look not into the heavens but into the future. Come now, point the telescope out the window, where day is just about to break.

Faust and Mephistopheles go to the window, and Faust gazes into the telescope.

M. You are looking far into the future. Over five centuries forward. The next five hundred years will be a time of great enlightenment for humanity. Gradually, through both terrible and noble struggles, humanity will grow up into a greater and greater knowledge. As the Scriptures say, they have grown up into the full humanity of Christ.

F. Christ? Did you say Christ?

M. Yes. Not the crude carpenter from Nazareth, but the true Christ—exalted humanity. Humanity with full knowledge of good and evil.

F. Ah yes. I see it now. Christ is the enlightened one!

M. The Christ within each individual is the true light that has come into the world. Did He not teach us, "The kingdom of god is within you"?

F. It has always been there.

M. Indeed. It is there waiting to be discovered. "Ask and you shall receive. Seek and you shall find."

F. "Knock and the door will be opened." It is the woman searching for the lost coin, the shepherd looking for the lost sheep.

M. These are the true Christians, are they not? The ones who have gone on the quest to find their own truth:

the truth within? They have grown up and achieved full knowledge. These are our brothers, yours and mine. They are the ones who will make great strides until they control all knowledge of this material realm. The truth (whatever that is) will be the truth they themselves create. Science will prevail. Great inventions that you cannot imagine will dominate the whole world. What do you see? Is it coming into focus?

F. I see people hurrying to and fro, but I cannot tell if they are men or women.

M. Yes. They dress alike. They have moved beyond male and female distinctions. They choose their own identity. They make themselves according to their own imagination and desire. This new humanity will have moved beyond Adam and Eve to become united in a new equality. It is the abolition of man. The old Adam dies so the new Everyman, who is no man, might live. Did not the apostle say, "In Christ there is neither male nor female?" Now, what else do you see?

F. Great metal birds. Man-made flying machines! Boxes on wheels that move by themselves, racing here and there on endless stone highways! Where are the horses? Can man endure such speeds? Is it possible?

M. With science, all things are possible.

F. The light! I see great cities. Towers of glass and iron filled with light. I see cities of light. Where does the light come from?

M. By that time, they will have harnessed the power of lightning and will have used that power to drive every sort of machine — but, most of all, machines that control their world.

F. How can such things be? I see each man and woman staring at a small rectangle of light in their hand. What is it? Each person seems hypnotized by the rectangle of light.

M. Those are the thinking machines that control them. The machines are connected invisibly. They use the machines to gather information, to entertain them and keep them satisfied in every way. Their lords and masters use the machines to watch over them and control their every action.

F. How so? How can they control the whole world?

M. Through knowledge. The masters of the machines control all knowledge. They gather all knowledge. They store all knowledge on the machines, and with these machines they manipulate history. They write it as they wish it to have been and not as it is. The masters of the machines have become omniscient, and with omniscience comes omnipotence.

F. I see no disease, suffering, violence, or strife. Have they eliminated all these terrible things?

M. They have eliminated disease. They have eliminated poverty, war, and violence. They have created a new Eden—a world where it is possible for all who wish it to enjoy supreme happiness. Is this not a noble goal? For all to be truly happy? To eradicate suffering?

F. How is it possible? How have they done such things?

M. Through knowledge. They have identified what makes a person violent, indigent, and dull, and they have eliminated them. They have eliminated the weak, the sick, the insane, and the disabled. They have bred a master race—a race to dominate the world, and, in

so doing, they have created the human soul: the immortal ones.

F. The vision is fading. It is gone. It was a dream. Such a
future is impossible.

They return to their chairs and continue to drink wine.

M. I assure you, my friend. It is not impossible. It is simply
a fruit that must ripen. Already the seeds have been
planted. Our friend Dr. Luther has opened the eyes
of many. For this new world order to come about, the
old order must pass away. And, alas, that cannot take
place without a certain amount of strife, but you must
understand that disorder is not evil. Progress emerges
from the great struggle.

F. Mankind is noble and great, but men are stupid and
stubborn. They distrust new knowledge and new ways.
Will there not be resistance to this future?

M. You forget. What you have seen is five hundred years in
the future. There will be wars and rumors of wars, but
then the end will come—the glorious end. Eventually,
everyone will come to the point of enlightenment you
have already reached. They will realize that there is
no "Heavenly Father"—no Heaven or Hell, angels
or demons. Science will prevail. The inventions that
come from science will improve their lives so greatly
that they will not need to argue about the existence
of God. They will simply have forgotten that He even
existed.

F. But the priests. The bishops. The Church. Surely they
and their beliefs will not disappear.

M. They, too, will be transformed. Scientific knowledge
will help them to see that the true strength of religion

is to help mankind ascend to his full potential. Rather than being in bondage to meaningless beliefs and ancient religious rules, each individual will discover his own true inner self. Religion will become what it always should have been: a practical set of rules for the humans to obey and a method to build up their self-assurance. It will help them gain true enlightenment and build a secure, prosperous, and happy life for all. Is this not the promise of the Prophet from Nazareth? "I have come to bring you life that is more abundant"?

F. The morning is breaking. I do not know why you have come, but I welcome you. I must think about this vision and all you have said about the human soul. I believe you have given me some answers.

M. But I would like to give you many more answers. I would like to grant you the full knowledge I have spoken about. For this great future to happen, we need more pioneers. We need learned, intelligent, sensitive men to forge the way and lead humanity to full knowledge and this new world of promise.

F. I am willing. As you have said, we are already kindred spirits. I understand all that you have said, but surely there is some price, some investment, some effort I must make?

M. Well now, you know the old tales. Even that foolish Rabbi from Nazareth was given the choice. If you would be my disciple, then you will gain the whole world. You will receive all knowledge, and from that you will enjoy wealth, pleasure, and power. But what sort of choice is this? You must give up your soul? It is an old wives' tale. We have already agreed on that point. You don't have a soul to give up. The bargain is empty. The point is moot. I demand nothing from you. You have nothing to lose and everything to gain. As we have seen, you will not "sacrifice your soul," for you have none. Instead, you will gain a soul as you advance toward true enlightenment.

F. And in gaining a true soul, I will help to bring about this future you have shown me?

M. Yes. A future that rewrites the past ... a future in which the whole of humanity will also have evolved to their full potential—in which the whole of humanity will also develop an immortal soul and live forever.

F. And if I accept your offer, I will live forever?

M., *putting his arm around Dr Faust's shoulder*. You will! I promise it! You will indeed live with me forever.

Part 2

The Way of Creative Subversion

Introduction to the Solution

The Slippery Serpent

In *Perelandra*—the second of C. S. Lewis' science fiction trilogy—the hero, Professor Ransom, has been transported to the planet Venus, which is still reveling in Edenic innocence.

Ransom encounters not only Venus's Eve but Venus's tempter, in the form of a scientist from earth—Professor Weston. In their first conversation, Weston spouts a progressive, pseudo-spiritual, intellectual load of mumbo jumbo about mankind living in harmony with one another and nature. It's the usual diabolical lie—all false promises and lofty dreams—and when Ransom punctures Weston's pomposity with the pin of common sense and the razor of philosophical steel, Weston responds with condescending arrogance before changing the subject.

As Weston descends first into madness, and then into demonic possession, his temptation of the lady of Venus becomes ever more subtle and emotive. He plays on her vanity. He seduces her to disobedience with the high drama that she would be a brave pioneer, taking hold of her own freedom in order to achieve full maturity. Most of all, he wears her down with endless discussion and "dialogue." He never rests until he gets her to give in. He bats away Ransom's objections with non sequiturs, mockery, ad hominem attacks, and outright lies.

Ransom expresses his frustration at the fact that the devil can fight dirty, but he can't. He also observes that the creature "used plenty of subtlety and intelligence when talking to the Lady, but ... that it regarded intelligence simply and solely as a weapon, which it had no more wish to employ in its off duty hours than a soldier has to do bayonet practice when he is on leave. Thought was for it a device necessary to certain ends, but thought in itself did not interest it."[44]

I have found the same to be increasingly true in any discussion not only with indoctrinated progressives but with ordinary folks. The discussion may concern politics, religion, sexuality, economics, or cultural matters. If there is a disagreement, there is very little logical thought or rational debate. The two isms of sentimentalism and pragmatism usually rule the day.

No true debate takes place. Instead, arguments are dismissed by changing the subject, launching a personal attack, or playing the victim. The invitation to "dialogue" is used as a weapon to wear a person down. There is no real wish to have an honest exchange of ideas. The more intellectual, like Lewis's demon-possessed Weston, use rational arguments not as a process to discover the truth but as a weapon — and a weapon that is more like a bludgeon than a rapier. If their intellectual argument falls flat, they simply deny, lie, and shout more loudly.

We shouldn't pretend this battle is new. In fact, the battle with the multiheaded Hydra is as old as Eden, but in our age, the serpent has assumed a new and frightening level of global strength.

[44] C. S. Lewis, *Perelandra* (New York: Scribner, 1972), 110.

The Beast from the East

I will tell you about a vision I once had. I hesitate to call it a "vision" because it makes me sound like some sort of Marian mystic. Probably better to call it a "mental image" or a "dream image."

It came to me in that in-between state when I was not sure if I was praying or dozing. But it really doesn't matter. What matters is the content and context of the vision.

It took place in November 1989, when the world was excited about the fall of the Berlin Wall. For those who don't remember, the Berlin Wall was the brutal, barbed-wire-topped barrier that was built across the city of Berlin to separate the communist Eastern part of the city from the free, democratic Western part of the city.

Across Europe, communism was crumbling, and my dream vision was this: I saw a gigantic brown bear lumbering along at great speed. It was terrifying—with red eyes and an open, slavering mouth with sharp teeth and blood dripping from its muzzle. It came to a crumbling wall and clambered over it. The bear had been the symbolic beast for Russia (as the eagle is for the United States), and I understood that the bear—the beast from the East—was the spirit of atheism and that, as communism crumbled, this beast was moving into new territory, from the East to the West.

I have thought much about that dream vision over the last twenty-five years, and it seems to me that my vision was prophetic. In those twenty-five years, we have seen in the West what can only be described as our own form of violent, virulent atheism. Not only have the "New Atheists" come about during that time, but many more-implicit forms of atheism have grown among us like a noxious cancer. These are the sixteen isms I have outlined in the first part of this book. Each of them is a manifestation of atheism. Our materialistic atheism is not enforced with secret police, confiscation of church property, imprisonment, and torture, as it was in the Soviet Union and Eastern Europe. Instead, it pervades every aspect of our Western culture.

Swimming in the Swamp

There is an old saying, "The last thing the fish sees is the water." We are the fish. The sixteen atheistic isms are the water—water that is murky and saturated with sewage and mud. These false, interlocking philosophies have not just influenced our culture. They *are* our culture. Because they are so foundational, we are unaware of them and underestimate their influence. Because we underestimate them, we have no real idea how to combat them.

Why is this? Because atheistic relativism has eaten away people's ability to have any kind of real discussion at all. If there is no such thing as truth, the argument simply slips and slides away. As I've said before, arguing with a relativist is like wrestling with an octopus in oil in the dark.

Because of relativism, the discussion will ultimately be driven by the other isms: sentimentalism, utilitarianism, pragmatism, and individualism. Any attempt to assess the truth or state a truth that may be binding will simply be shrugged off: "You have your truth, and I have mine."

Carl Trueman points out that debate is not only difficult but impossible. Two people who agree that there is an ultimate foundation of truth that is beyond their experience have a basis for discussion. If one side believes in a greater source of truth, however, and the other not only denies it but doesn't even have a concept of a transcendent source of truth, debate is dead. There is no connection. They are playing tennis on adjacent courts.[45]

---

[45] Trueman, *The Rise and Triumph*, 80–81.

This is the situation we are in as Christian believers in twenty-first-century Western society. We believe in a transcendent foundation of truth. The majority of Americans either deny the existence of this greater authority or are ignorant of it altogether. Many of those who call themselves Christians — even among our Christian leaders — deny this greater authority or at least deny its relevance to everyday matters. This is why so many of the arguments in the culture wars are like Ransom's argument with Weston. It's as pointless and ridiculous as a terrier growling and chewing and shaking a slipper.

What can be done? How can a battle even commence? How can one even attempt to behead this creature from the black lagoon — this Hydra from the swamp?

Conflict, Engagement, or Retreat

In the first part of this book, I grouped the isms in the categories of the world, the flesh, and the devil because Jesus Christ Himself encountered temptations in these categories in the desert. We who are His disciples have continued to battle these isms down through the centuries — albeit in different forms and with different emphases.

It is worth pausing to consider how our ancestors did battle because, just as the enemy is subtle, the weapons for battle are not what you might expect. In *Rethinking the Enlightenment*, Joseph Stuart discusses how Christians engaged the anti-Christian philosophies in the eighteenth century. They went to war in three ways: conflict, engagement, and retreat.

The first, conflict, is a full one-on-one, head-to-head battle. Down through history, this has sometimes meant not only an intellectual and political power struggle but actual warfare, persecution, and bloodshed. This was a failure. It was counterproductive

and only made the enemies of the truth resentful and more determined to fight back harder next time.

The second method, engagement, was accommodation. In
every age, what seems to be a "good Christian" approach to Satan's lies is to find what seems good within the opposing side's
position. It seems as if the most reasonable way forward is to
dialogue — to reason with the opposition and, through negotia-
tion and listening, to find shared values and a middle ground of
tolerance and cooperation.

Although this sounds good, inevitably it, too, fails because
it weakens the Faith. Resolve disintegrates, and the enemies of
truth gain ground. Moreover, as I have pointed out above, we
are in a new situation; the isms have prevailed to such an extent
that there is no shared foundation and therefore no realistic basis
for dialogue.

Furthermore, atheistic relativists regard those with a transcendent worldview as dangerous bullies who want to impose their
faith along with its pointless restrictions on everyone. Dialogue?
The enemies of the Catholic Faith are not interested in dialogue,
and they are certainly not interested in compromise. They do
not intend to take prisoners. If you give them an inch, they will
take ten miles, and Catholics who believe otherwise are naïve.
Christians who seek to accommodate the ways of the world end
up adopting the ways of the world, and inevitably the Faith
becomes watered down, the Church is weakened, and the light
of Christ grows dim.

Conflict or accommodation has been the Catholic Church's
experience throughout the nineteenth and twentieth centuries.
Popes Pius IX and Pius X fought hard to suppress liberalism and
modernism. They entered the conflict, and through their encycli-
cals, the oath against modernism, the Index of Forbidden Books,

and a determined enforcement of rules and regulations, they tried to defeat the lies, but the heads of the Hydra would not be defeated. The serpents of modernism simply slithered away and hid.

The second Vatican Council can be understood as an attempt at accommodation. The Fathers of the Council tried a different tactic. They studied carefully and selected what they thought was good from the modern world and adapted those ideas to Church teaching. The Second Vatican Council was a great experiment in engagement, ecumenism, and encouragement, but as we have all experienced, it left the Faith weakened. The enemies of the Church were given an inch, and they used "the spirit of Vatican II" to take ten thousand miles. Vocations to the priesthood and religious life plummeted, attendance at Mass nosedived, and thousands of Catholics left the Church for Protestant churches, other religions, or nothing at all.

Stuart calls the third method of dealing with the lies of the Enlightenment period "retreat." I prefer the term "creative subversion." Stuart uses the example from the eighteenth century of the Great Awakening and the Methodist revival. Charles and John Wesley were Oxford educated. They were well aware of the anti-Christian intellectual trends of the eighteenth century. The Wesley brothers just went around them.

They did not engage in open conflict, nor did they accommodate the Enlightenment philosophies and compromise their faith. Instead, they simply got on with the task of living radical, dynamic, obedient, Spirit-filled lives. They evangelized the working classes. They wrote books and hymns. They traveled tirelessly, preaching the gospel. They started churches, ran Bible studies, advised the poor, organized charities to battle against poverty and alcoholism, started schools, campaigned against social injustice, and raised money for all the good work they were doing.

Beheading Hydra

They may not have been Catholics, but they were Christian heroes, and the Catholics who have done the same down the ages — the apostles and early believers, the Benedictine monks, the Jesuit missionary martyrs, and countless others — realized that the best strategy was simply to sidestep the subtle lies, roll up their sleeves, and do what they could where they were and with what they had.

Hercules the Hero

Did I say there was a Hydra? There was also a hero. His name was Hercules, and he was sent by the gods to kill the dreaded serpent of the swamps of Lerna. In the second part of the book, we will look again at the sixteen isms and learn the practical steps we can take to overcome them.

Some members of the Body of Christ might choose to engage in direct conflict with the sixteen isms, and others might choose to accommodate, dialogue, and reason with the followers of the way of the world. I believe both of these attempts will founder and fail. Instead, the right way to counter the lies is the third way — the way of creative subversion.

It is not only better to light a candle than to curse the dark, but it is also the only way to banish the dark. Only by the light of our lives will we defeat the darkness. Debate and dialogue now are pointless. Our lives must be our argument. Is it still a battle? To be sure; and engaging in battle by living radiant, Spirit-filled lives is the most effective way to engage in the combat.

Every Five Hundred Years

This has happened time and again over the two-thousand-year history of the Church: the Church has descended into heresy, corruption, and immorality, and society has fallen into decadence, despair, vice, and violence. That is when ordinary men and women rise up and become extraordinary heroes. They are given the grace to see the problem clearly and understand the solutions.

Every five hundred years, there seems to be a major crisis in the Faith, and at each juncture, a new wave of witnesses rise up.

Ancient Rome was a cruel, dark, and demon-possessed society, but Rodney Stark has shown how the first Christians simply lived a graced life of charity and peace, and the pagan world was drawn to their example and converted.[46]

At the beginning of the sixth century, the Church was listless and corrupt, and the Roman Empire had crumbled into chaos and anarchy. St. Benedict stepped out and established simple communities centered on prayer, work, and reading, thereby planting the seeds out of which a new Christendom blossomed.

By the turn of the first millennium, Church and society had once more drifted into corruption, crime, sin, decadence, and complacency. The Benedictine Order surged forth in the great Cistercian renewal. This was a fresh wave of monastic missionary effort that brought an amazing resurgence of Christian learning, culture, and faith.

Five hundred years later, the Church had again drifted into corruption, and society was broken into chaos and confusion. This time, it was the saints of the Counter-Reformation who brought renewal simply by living out the creatively subversive alternative.

Another five hundred years has passed. We now stand on a new threshold. It is our turn. But this time it is different. We have drifted into the swamp before, but I believe we are now

---

[46] Rodney Stark, *Cities of God: The Real Story of How Christianity Became an Urban Movement and Conquered Rome* (New York: HarperOne, 2009).

facing a battle in the world and the Church that the world has never seen before.

The human race has never before existed in a culture without any kind of transcendent points of reference.[47] In the previous conflicts — even with bitter disagreements — there has been a shared foundation — a shared belief in an authority that was greater than the material realm. Then both combatants had ground on which to stand. Now we are in a new kind of wasteland. We are dancing on quicksand — standing on the edge of a "grimpen where there is no secure foothold, and menaced by monsters."[48]

A Counterfeit Faith

Furthermore, I am convinced that this message is not denominational. The Christian church today is not divided into Eastern Orthodox, Catholic, and Protestant. It is divided into those who believe in the core Christian faith and those who follow a counterfeit version of Christianity.

This false version of Christianity turns the supernatural religion of the Cross and the Resurrection into a formula of good works to make people respectable. It adds an attractive stream of therapy to make people superficially happy and tops it off with a vague belief in God as "the spiritual dimension within." This fake religion gives the whole scam the appearance of true religion. Jesus, in this fake religion, is a nice guy, a wise teacher, a gentle soul, a spiritual guide, a community organizer, a social justice warrior, and a caring healer. But he's not the incarnate Son of God, the second Person of the Holy and Undivided Trinity, who

---

[47] Trueman, *The Rise and Triumph*, 74–77.
[48] Eliot, *The Waste Land*, 125.

took flesh of the Blessed Virgin Mary, His Mother. He's not the Lamb of God who takes away the sins of the world. He's not the Redeemer of mankind, who shed His blood on the old, rugged Cross and then rose again to banish death forever.

Those who believe and attempt to live authentic, Christianity do so within Eastern Orthodoxy, Catholicism, and Protestantism. Despite our differences in customs and doctrines, we share in a core belief that the Christian faith is supernaturally revealed by God and that its fundamental tenets and moral teachings cannot be changed. It is we who need to be changed.

Those who follow the religion of the antichrist believe the Christian faith is a human construct derived from a particular culture that is not revealed but relative. The doctrines of this religion are the sixteen heads of the Hydra that I have exposed, but the beast of Lerna is in our churches. The Hydra heads wear bishops' miters, and the dragons are clothed in the rich robes of popular priests, the academic gowns of theology professors, the sober suits of Protestant pastors, and the sleek suits of prosperity-gospel preachers.

Genuine disagreements on doctrine remain between Catholics, Protestants, and the Eastern Orthodox, and these cannot be ignored, but the deepest divide in Christendom is between those who follow the core gospel and those who follow the gospel of the antichrist. Archbishop Fulton Sheen predicted the rise of this counterfeit Christianity—the religion of the antichrist:

> This is the temptation to have a new religion without a Cross, a liturgy without a world to come, a religion to destroy a religion, or a politics which is a religion—one that renders unto Caesar even the things that are God's.

In the midst of all his seeming love for humanity and his glib talk of freedom and equality, he will have one great secret which he will tell to no one: he will not believe in God. Because his religion will be brotherhood of Man without the fatherhood of God, he will deceive even the elect. He will set up a counter church which will be the ape of the Church, because he, the Devil, is the ape of God. It will have all the notes and characteristics of the Church, but in reverse and emptied of its divine content. It will be a mystical body of the Antichrist that will in all externals resemble the mystical body of Christ.[49]

Notice that this false religion is not organized into a denomination with a recognizable infrastructure, creed, and hierarchy. Instead, it is a transdenominational, interfaith infestation. Like an intestinal worm, this false religion works its way into the guts of all the Christian denominations. It distorts and destroys them from within. This religion of the antichrist infects and feeds on all the churches like a hideous parasite, but one that manifests itself with a smile.

This seductive spirit appeals to weak Christians of sentimental faith and shallow catechesis. The counterfeit faith is hard to resist because it presents itself as gentle, kind, tolerant, and unifying. Resist this sly beast with the kindly face, and you will be blamed, vilified, and castigated as unloving, divisive, judgmental, and unkind. You'll be blamed for being the worst kind of repressive, legalistic, and dictatorial fundamentalist Pharisee.

---

[49] Fulton Sheen, *Communism and the Conscience of the West* (Pekin, IN: Refuge of Sinners Publishing, 1948), 63.

A Radical Plan

The word radical comes from the Latin word for "root." To be radical is to go back to the roots—to be rooted—and in this chaotic, fast-swirling society, to be rooted in any belief system at all is to be a bewildering presence. Just as, in a world of fugitives, the one who goes home will seem to be running away, so, in a world of anarchy, to be "rooted and grounded in love" (Eph. 3:17) is to be subversive, and to live this life joyfully and positively is to be what Pope Benedict XVI called a "creative minority."

What I propose is no less than the radical discipleship of the first Christians in the Roman Empire, the creative subversion of St. Benedict and his disciples, the innovative and dynamic example of the Cistercian reform, the admirable qualities of Protestant zeal, and the Catholic Reformation. In every age, Christians have followed the Lord Jesus Christ, who, by His own example, taught how to be a force of creative subversion in the world.

So, with whatever gifts we have, we will step out in faith to follow Christ in radical discipleship. We will step out with great courage to wield the sword of truth and the fire of love and do battle with the Hydra. Then, by the grace given to us, and from our obedience and sacrifice, the Hydra will be beheaded and the seeds planted for a new civilization of love and light to flourish.

10

Your Money or Your Life

Tithing and Prayer versus Materialism and Atheism
Often when I am taking questions at a speaking engagement, someone will ask, "What can we do to make sure our kids stay Catholic?"

I reply, "Do you really want to know what I think? You're not going to like my answer."

"Yes, of course. What do you think will help keep our kids Catholic?"

"Tithe. Give at least 10 percent of your money away."

At this point, the questioner looks rather sad, and I reply, "I said you wouldn't like my answer."

Tithing is the way to behead the first Hydra head, materialism. When you tithe, you are cutting off the head of materialism, because materialism is the philosophy that this physical, material world is all there is. Money is the tangible expression of a materialist philosophy because money is how we buy more stuff and gain more power. When we put money and material possessions first in our lives, we are affirming a materialistic worldview. When we give generously, we are subverting that worldview in a positive, creative way.

Because our money and our possessions are the manifestation of the material world, what we do with our money and our possessions is a sign of our true beliefs. Jesus said it Himself: "No one can serve two masters. He will either hate one and love the other, or be devoted to one and despise the other. You cannot serve God and mammon" (Matt. 6:24). By tithing you show your money who's boss and prove that you love God, not money.

Now, perhaps you are squirming. You have agreed with my assessment of the sixteen heads of the Hydra, and you have said in your head that you want to do battle against them, but now, when I say that the first step is to tithe, you pull back. You make excuses. You chicken out.

The battle is real. Reading a book about the battle is easy, but it is not the battle. The battle involves real actions by real people. Can you begin this battle by seeing that it has to do with something as basic and real as your money?

Is money the root of all evil? No. The Scriptures say the *love* of money is the root of all evil (1 Tim. 6:10). Furthermore, the same verse goes on to say that, by coveting money, many have departed from the Faith. In other words, there is a spiritual price to pay for the love of money; but when you tithe, you receive a spiritual bonus, and you slice off that head of the Hydra with a vengeance.

We're called to be happy warriors. The Bible also says, "Whoever sows sparingly will also reap sparingly, and whoever sows bountifully will also reap bountifully. Each must do as already determined, without sadness or compulsion, for God loves a cheerful giver" (2 Cor. 9:6–7).

Giving generously is liberating because it frees us from our bondage to money and therefore from the curse of materialism.

As we invest in the work of the Church, in charity to the needy and to educational institutions, we are saying, "Yes! *This* is what I believe in. *This* is an eternal investment. I believe in the spiritual realm so much that I'm putting my money where my mouth is. Furthermore, I am doing so sacrificially and joyfully."

Keep Your Kids Christian

There were five kids in our family. My dad had his own men's clothing store. We went to church every Sunday. My dad taught Sunday school and was an elder in the church. He also gave 15 percent of his income (before taxes) to the Lord's work. He did this even when his business was failing and he had three kids in college.

For an economics class when I was in eighth grade, I had to create a pie chart showing my family's income and expenditure. While I was working on it, the teacher walked down the aisle and looked over my shoulder. He said, "Dwight, I think you made a mistake here. You put down 15 percent of your family's income being given to charity. I think you meant to put 1.5 percent."

"No, sir," I said. "My dad gives 15 percent of our money to the church." I was so proud. I still get a lump in my throat when I remember this.

One of the reasons I am still a believer is that I knew that my father put his money where his mouth was. He wasn't perfect, but he tithed—even when it was difficult. He lived his faith, and by that example, he taught me and the whole world that he did not live by the philosophy of materialism.

Matter Matters

It is vital to understand our true relationship to the material world. God has created us with physical bodies and put us in a physical world. Furthermore, He did not create junk. He stepped out and viewed His creation and said, "That's good!"

The seventeenth-century poet Thomas Traherne wrote, "Can a man be just unless he love all things according to their worth?"[50] We are called, therefore, to do just that: to love all things according to their worth. The trick is to assess their truth worth properly.

The true worth of a house, for example, is that it is a dwelling place. It provides warmth, welcome, and security for a family. It also provides long-term financial security as an investment. This is what a house is for. That is its worth. To love a house because it is in a swanky neighborhood, however, or to want a house that is far larger than we need in order to show off, or to have lots of houses in order to become obscenely rich: all these are vanity, pride, and greed and therefore not loving the house according to its worth.

The way to love all things according to their worth is by getting our priorities right. This is the proper understanding of detachment. For most people, detachment cannot be absolute poverty but, instead, should be a right ordering of our loves. By tithing we are putting things in their right order. When we do this, everything else falls into line. "seek first the kingdom [of God] and his righteousness, and all these things will be given you besides" (Matt. 6:33).

In recommending tithing, I suggest that you set a percentage of your family income that you can afford to give. If you are clearing debt and have overwhelming financial responsibilities, your percentage may be lower than the typical 10 percent. If your income level is higher and you have been blessed, however, your tithing should be boosted to as big a percentage as you can afford. The general guideline is that you should tithe enough so that it hurts at least a little. If it doesn't bite back, you're not really attacking the head of the Hydra!

[50] Thomas Traherne, *Centuries of Meditations*, private publication.

Fighting Atheism

The second head of the Hydra is atheism. You'll remember from chapter 1 that materialism is simply a mask of atheism. If you believe only in the material world and deny the existence of a spiritual realm, then, by definition, you do not believe in God, who is the ultimate invisible reality.

Like the other heads of the Hydra, atheism in our society is rarely mentioned. Nevertheless, our culture is deeply atheistic. Furthermore, many materialistic atheists go to church. The American form of materialistic atheism is not the militant kind that surfaced in China or Soviet Russia. This materialistic atheism does not persecute Christians (at least not yet); instead, it sits comfortably in the pews of the mainstream Christian churches.

How does one battle against this soft and sweet version of atheism? Once again, a direct attack does not work; neither does accommodation. The direct attack would be brushed aside with a patronizing comment. Dialogue will serve only to waste time and weaken the true Faith.

The answer to American atheism is prayer — real, fervent, disciplined, life-changing prayer. Why is prayer the answer? Because when we pray, we are taking action against the atheism that denies the existence of the spiritual realm. In prayer, we are not making intellectual arguments against atheism. Instead, through prayer, we are opening the gates of grace and plugging into the power source of the cosmos.

When we pray, we are saying, "God's power is at work in the world, and I'm joining my will and my life with this great force. This power is like the sea, and I'm surfing. I'm plunging in and paddling out into the depths, and then I'm getting up in a moment of daring and skill to ride the waves of grace. Try to stop me!"

How do we pray? No one can do the work of praying for you, and no one can really teach you to pray. It is like surfing or like riding a bike. A teacher can show you the basics and give you an example, but you have to get up on the board, get up on the bike, and get going. Furthermore, as with surfing or riding a bike, once you get the hang of it, you can always do it.

The Church provides the tools — the liturgy, the various forms of spirituality, the examples of the saints, and umpteen books and websites and courses on prayer — but this is an action you must do to counter not only the atheism in the world but also the atheism in your own heart.[51]

Facing Facts

"But I'm not an atheist!" I hear you say. Really? Then why do you live like one? If you do not pray, if you do not tithe, if you are living without a real relationship with God, then your belief in God is only a theory. Maybe it is only a theory that you never bothered even to think about or challenge. If so, then you are also one of the default atheists. You would never be so bold as to claim the title and wear it as a badge of honor, but you live like an atheist.

Think for a moment what it would be like if just 10 percent of those who call themselves Christians lived like Christians. What would our world be like if we beheaded the Hydra of materialism by giving generously and cut off the head of atheism by lives dedicated to prayer? If even a small minority of Christians lived like this, the tide would be turned and the world would be changed.

---

[51] Chapter 3 of John Senior's *The Restoration of Christian Culture* contains an excellent encouragement to disciplined and organized prayer.

If that creative minority of Christians really took these actions, the corruption in the Church would shrivel up. The immorality in the Church would be exposed and die of shame. The weakness, lassitude, and discouragement in the Church would disappear. Vocations would burgeon again, and faith would spring up in confidence because ordinary men and women would have had the courage to do battle in practical ways by undermining the insidious materialism and atheism of our age.

11

Presence, Providence, and Power

Sacraments and Scripture versus
Scientism and Historicism

When I was a young Anglican priest, I was asked to accompany an older priest, Fr. Philip, to anoint a woman who was suffering from cancer. Having been brought up in a conservative Evangelical family, I was cynical about the healing ministry. To my mind, faith healers were hucksters who would weep and plead for your twenty-dollar donation and then wave their arms about and pretend to heal you.

My training in a Church of England seminary at Oxford was rooted in historical Anglican Protestant theology. For Evangelical Anglicans, the sacraments are more than mere symbols, but not much more. As low-church Anglicans, we considered the sacraments to be "means of grace" in a general, spiritual way. Furthermore, we were taught that there were only two sacraments: Baptism and Holy Communion.

In my first few years of ministry, when I began working with Anglo-Catholic priests, I also began to accept a more Catholic understanding of the sacraments. Still, being invited to conduct a service of prayer, laying on of hands, and anointing of the sick, I was skeptical. The day before the appointment, I tried to back out.

I said to Fr. Philip, "I can't heal anyone. I'm not a faith healer."

"Of course you're not," he replied. "Christ is the healer. But He can heal through you."

"But what if we anoint this person and nothing happens?"

Fr. Philip's eyes lit up with enthusiasm and faith. "Oh, don't worry about that. Something *always* happens. We just can't predict what it is."

The next day, Fr. Philip and I prayed together, laid hands on the woman, prayed for healing, and anointed her, and she experienced a remission from her cancer. Over the years, I have found Fr. Philip's words to echo true time and again: in the sacraments, something always happens.

Sometimes the healing is physical and seemingly miraculous. Sometimes there is a psychological healing, a healing of relationships, or simply a release from guilt, fear, and anxiety. Other times the people receiving the sacraments will go through surgery and treatment with very little pain, or if they are at the end of their lives, go through the portal of death with great peace and often with a surge of joy and confidence.

I went forward in faith and accepted a new understanding of the sacraments, and this is the answer to the ideology of scientism.

The Real Presence

Scientism, you'll remember, is the logical conclusion of materialism. If the physical, material world is all there is, then the only source of knowledge is the analysis and measurement of the physical world though science. If there is an immaterial, invisible dimension to reality, however, there must be not only a link between the physical and the spiritual but also a way to experience that link and open the door between the two realms; otherwise the idea of an invisible realm remains just a fanciful idea.

The Catholic Church practices the only real answer to scientism. Scientism says there is only this material, physical realm. Catholicism says the spiritual power works in and through the physical. God's invisible grace and goodness flow through the sacramental actions of Christ in His Church.

Something always happens.

If you are a non-Catholic Christian reading this book, I am not saying your faith is worthless because you deny the reality of the Catholic sacraments. I am simply saying that, instead of "mere Christianity," you might think about exploring the "more Christianity" of Catholicism.[52]

When we enter a Catholic Church, we are blessed to see the red sanctuary light burning. This is a powerful sign of our belief as Catholics—a belief that no one has in the same way—the belief that Jesus Christ is really present in the sacrament of the altar and that His presence is *not* just symbolic. That sacramental presence in the tabernacle is a reminder that what was once bread and wine is now the Body and Blood of Christ. How it is His Real Presence is worth reviewing. Let me explain:

In one of our rooms at home, we have a collection of family photographs. There is one there of me at the age of eighteen months in my father's arms. There is also a family photo of me at the age of ten. My high school graduation picture is there, as well as pictures of me at grad school, getting married, and being ordained, and a picture from just last year. In each photograph, my physical body is different, but in each photograph we can also see the same Dwight Longenecker. That same person is the eternal part of me. It is the real me. It is my soul, if you like.

---

[52] See Dwight Longenecker, *More Christianity* (San Francisco: Ignatius Press, 2010).

It is this real but invisible aspect of the bread and wine we say is transformed into the Body and Blood of Christ. We refer to this eternal, unchanging dimension of a thing as its *substance*, and it is this substance of the bread and wine that is changed — thus giving us the term "transubstantiation."

To grasp this transformation is to understand and accept a sacramental vision of the world — not just the transformation of bread and wine but, through the use of physical means, the transformation of the whole world. To have this sacramental vision is to see the invisible power of God active and surging in the created world at all times and in all places — but becoming focused and particular through the sacraments of the Church.

Scientism or Sacramentalism

Scientism contends that the physical realm can be understood only by analyzing the material aspect. Sacramentalism says it is that very physical, material world through which God interacts and connects with humanity, and only through a fully sacramental experience can one come not only to know the spiritual realm but also to understand fully the significance of the physical realm.

I realize that Protestants who hold to the core beliefs of the historical faith are our brothers and sisters, and their continued belief in miracles and the supernatural dimension of the Faith is important to acknowledge, but it is also crucial to understand that this real link between this world and the next was broken at the Protestant Revolution, and this denial of the sacramental reality is one of the contributing factors to the growth of rationalism, materialism, and scientism in the world.

With the denial of the sacraments, the living link between Heaven and earth was broken, and humanity went down the path of materialism, atheism, and all the other heads of the Hydra we have considered.

What does this mean in everyday life? It means that we live in a constant awareness of God's supernatural presence in our lives, and we live in a constant expectation of His grace flowing to us through the sacraments. We say that the sacraments "effect what they signify." In Fr. Philip's words, "Something always happens."

In Baptism, my sins are washed away. In Confirmation, I really am strengthened by the Holy Spirit. In Confession, my sins really are forgiven, and in the Anointing of the Sick, I am truly healed. In Marriage and Ordination, my life is transformed from the inside out as I commit myself to a lifetime of loving service.

Living the sacramental life is an action and an attitude that conquers scientism. Living this Catholic life in a dynamic and positive way is not an intellectual argument against scientism. It is a life that is real and an encounter with the invisible realm that defeats scientism by its reality, not simply by a theory or a doctrine one affirms.

We too often think of the supernatural realm as "out there," as if the spiritual realm were up in the clouds. But the sacramental life makes us experience the truth that, while God is transcendent and "out there," He is also, because of Christ's Incarnation and the life of the Church, here with us—closer to us than our breath itself.

Providence and Power

Another powerful part of the Christian life severs the Hydra head of historicism. Historicism is the view that, if there is no God, then there is no overarching story of history. The events of history are simply random acts of power. If a vital life within the sacraments answers the emptiness of scientism, what is the answer to historicism?

This is where our Protestant brothers and sisters come into their own with their love of the Bible. The answer to historicism is to read and love the Sacred Scriptures.

Understand this: The Scriptures are not primarily a rule book. The Bible is not first and foremost a source to be mined for religious doctrine. It is not just a collection of wise sayings or a list of guidelines for a happy life. The Bible may contain all these things and be used for these purposes, but Sacred Scripture's primary role is the record of God's relationship with humanity. In other words, it is a history book.

From the beginning, in the Garden of Eden, to the final chapter of Revelation, the Bible lays out, step by step, God's unfolding relationship with mankind, and from the very beginning, the stories are presented as historical. This is the remarkable difference between the Judeo-Christian religion and every other religion. Other religions have spiritual teachings and myths about their gods and goddesses, but none of them tell the ongoing story of the creator God's fatherly relationship with a particular tribe of nomads, through whom He Himself eventually steps onto the stage of human history.

Historicism denies the existence of this overarching drama — this great saga of salvation. Therefore, to counter the emptiness of historicism, read the Bible; and because the Scriptures are supernaturally inspired (not just an ordinary human composition), by reading the Bible, you are cutting off the heads of both historicism and materialism at the same time. Study and read the Bible enthusiastically and intelligently. Use resources online — for instance, from the Augustine Institute, the St. Paul Center for

Biblical Studies, Catholic Productions, and Ascension Press. Learn the Bible timeline, and teach it to your children.

God's plan for humanity has continued through the life of the Church. Therefore, to counter historicism, read Church history in addition to the Sacred Scriptures. Read the lives of the saints. Trace the loving hand of God throughout the great drama of our race, and you will see and understand the ways of God in the world.

This will also help you to understand the truth that God is involved not only in human history but in *your* history. By coming to see how He works, you will understand better how He is involved in your life and in the life of your family.

Your understanding of God's relationship with the human family will merge with a sacramental vision for the world as you will come to recognize God's providence—God's plan as woven through every aspect of human history. You will see that God was there working through history's triumphs and the tragedies—never forsaking His people—His Holy Spirit never being spent, and that the world is always charged with God's grandeur. Thus, even through frail, stumbling history, God pours out His grace on us.

Scientism and Historicism Shrivel

With this kind of full vision of reality, scientism and historicism simply shrivel up and die for want of energy and purpose. In the face of a sacramental vision of reality, scientism is revealed for what it always was—a dull, barren, lifeless thing. Scientism is to sacramentalism what an autopsy is to the resurrection and the life.

In the face of a fully providential understanding of history, historicism is seen for what it really is: a hollow recitation of random events and their consequences. Providence, on the other hand, infuses every triumph and tragedy of history with the light of meaning and ultimate purpose.

This full-blooded participation in the sacraments and providence needs to be woven into the lives and vision of our families, our parishes, and our schools. At every opportunity, we should share the reality of God's working His will and way in the world — always and everywhere seeing His mighty hand in all His works and offering praise. This is not just a new way of seeing. It is a new way of being.

The Role of Worship

Remember, this is not just a theory. For the sacramental vision to have a full effect, it is put into action through worship. We have forgotten what the Mass and the administration of the sacraments are all about. We have taken a utilitarian approach — turning the Mass into a family fellowship time, treating Baptism as no more than a celebration of a child's birth. Confession has been turned into a form of therapy, Marriage no more than a sentimental celebration of a couple's love, and Confirmation an adolescent rite of passage.

The celebration of the sacraments includes these elements, but first and foremost, they are an activation of God's grace in our lives. The worship we offer is the context by which we connect with this supernatural power. The modernist church, however, has quietly removed this aspect of the sacraments, thus emasculating them for many people. Instead of an earthquake encounter with the living God, the sacraments have become no more than anodyne forms of therapy and community celebration.

In the liturgy, the sacraments and the history are put into action through worship. In the liturgy, we read and meditate on the Sacred Scriptures — the history of God's work in the world.

Did I say we need creatively subversive action in the world to counter the poison of the Hydra? The Mass is *God's* creatively subversive action in the world, and when we participate in the Mass, we join our action with His.

This attitude and this action on a weekly and daily basis counteract the debilitating and destructive attitude of scientism and historicism in our society; and as we live this kind of life, we offer a creatively subversive alternative: a life that is embedded in the supernatural realities of a God who is Emmanuel—God with us.

12

The Risk of Faith

Evangelization and Daring versus
Utilitarianism and Pragmatism

I was eighteen and in my senior year of high school when the Rev. Peter Deyneka visited. Deyneka was a burly Russian immigrant who founded a mission organization called Slavic Gospel Association. He was at our church to speak about his work and raise funds, and he was an overnight guest in our home.

Over dinner, he told us about his work smuggling Bibles and Christian literature into the communist countries of Eastern Europe. I was captivated by the thought of such an adventure. Then, over dessert, Rev. Deyneka (who was nicknamed "Peter Dynamite") said he was starting a summer mission team project. College students would live and work in France for the summer and take trips into communist countries, posing as tourists, with their camper van filled with boxes of Bibles.

Rev. Deyneka looked me straight in the eye and said, "Why don't you join the mission team this summer?" I gulped. "Who, me?" Immediately I came up with reasons why not. We had to raise the money to go on the trip. I didn't have any money. "God will provide" said Peter Dynamite.

So I sent in my application and wrote some begging letters. The night before I set off for Chicago to meet the rest of the mission team, I still needed $500.

I said to my dad, "I'll sell my motorcycle."

"Wait. God will provide." That evening, some friends came by to give me a graduation present. "Dwight, we were going to give you $250, but the Lord laid it on our heart to double it."

God provided. I went on the mission trip to smuggle Bibles into communist Russia and Eastern Europe.

Salvation or Happiness?

Why did we go to such lengths to smuggle Bibles into communist countries? For that matter, why do any missionaries risk all and sacrifice their lives to bring the gospel to those who have never heard of the Lord Jesus Christ? Missionaries do so because they believe in the invisible realm. They believe each human person has an eternal soul, and that soul is worth saving. They do so because it is through faith in the saving work of Christ on the Cross and baptism into his sacrifice that souls are rescued and redeemed.

This is the core of the Christian gospel, and it flies in the face of dull utilitarianism. The utilitarian atheist does not believe in the human soul, Heaven, Hell, or eternal life. As far as he is concerned, the only thing worth working for is happiness for the greatest number here and now.

Have you noticed how utilitarianism has infected the Church? Christians used to be missionaries. They built hospitals and schools, but first they preached the gospel, baptized converts, and built churches. Now they just build hospitals and schools and forget about the gospel. Why is that? Because utilitarianism is all about making this world a better place rather than about the salvation of souls.

Undermining Utilitarianism

We should never pull back from our commitment to serve the poor, the marginalized, and the needy, but if we want to cut off the head of utilitarianism, we will bring back an idea that is embarrassing and ridiculous to the worldly person—and to the worldly Christian—and that is evangelization.

Utilitarianism seeks the greatest happiness for the greatest number. The way to defeat this philosophy is to insist that the greatest happiness is eternal life and that, therefore, the greatest happiness for the greatest number means opening the door to eternal life to the greatest number of people.

Do you want to be creatively subversive? Talk about real, old-fashioned evangelization. Oh yes, everyone likes to use the buzzword of the "new evangelization," but few actually do it.

Pope Francis and Pope Benedict teach that the most effective evangelization is through attraction, not coercion. To put it simply, "Others should see how we live and say, 'I want what they have.'" Although this is the most powerful way to witness, real evangelization also needs to be pro-active, positive, and articulate. In fact, words and works go together. If we speak the gospel but do not live the gospel, our words are dead; but likewise, if we only live the gospel and never speak it, others will not hear the good news and believe. St. Paul Street Evangelization is a new Catholic apostolate that trains ordinary Catholics to share their Faith in ways that are positive and proactive.

Why does evangelization cut off the head of utilitarianism? Because to care about the eternal destiny of someone's soul, by very definition, undercuts utilitarianism, which focuses only on a person's happiness in this material realm.

God's Fools

The tag-team partner of utilitarianism is pragmatism — the desire to take practical, efficient, cost-effective measures without any thought of eternal ramifications or moral principles. The pragmatist is interested only in the bottom line. Because he is a materialist, he has no sense of a greater goal or an eternal purpose. He would hear Peter Deyneka say, "God will provide!" and say with a condescending smile, "Show me the balance sheet."

In chapter 3, I wrote about how the Church has been infected with pragmatism. The structures of the Church are too often run by men and women in gray suits. Behind the scenes, everything is controlled by the financiers, insurance companies, human-resource departments, accountants, and lawyers, who are naturally averse to any kind of risk.

The story is told of a wealthy Catholic who gave Mother Teresa a million dollars. She thanked him and said with that money she could open five new orphanages. He stopped her politely and said, "Mother, perhaps you do not understand the principles of wise financial management. If you invest that million dollars, you will have the income to run all your orphanages."

She gave him that famous squinty smile and said, "Perhaps you do not understand the principles of God's financial management. If I spend this million dollars to open five new orphanages, God will send five more wealthy people to give us a million dollars."

Of course, we need to be good stewards of God's resources, but God's principles of financial management are different from our worldly-wise principles. To be too careful is not the way of faith. St. Peter didn't put on a life jacket before he stepped out of the boat to walk on the waves.

Pilgrim John

Radical discipleship is the antidote to pragmatism. Jesus explains radical discipleship as he sends out His disciples:

> He summoned the Twelve and began to send them out two by two and gave them authority over unclean spirits. He instructed them to take nothing for the journey but a walking stick — no food, no sack, no money in their belts. They were, however, to wear sandals but not a second tunic. He said to them, "Wherever you enter a house, stay there until you leave from there. Whatever place does not welcome you or listen to you, leave there and shake the dust off your feet in testimony against them." (Mark 6:7–11)

My brother Don lives at the beach, and one day, he spotted a man with a long beard wearing what looked like a Franciscan habit. The man was barefoot but carried his sandals. He wore a small backpack, was using a long walking stick, and had a Bible tucked under his arm. My brother was intrigued and struck up a conversation.

It turned out that the beach walker used to be a New York stockbroker. His name was John, and he said, "I decided to take the Lord at his word and follow the gospel. I sold everything and set out with a stick, sandals, and my Bible and decided to just walk and meet people and share the gospel and ask them to repent."

"How do they take that?"

"Most people listen. Some cry. Others hug me. A few mock me. It doesn't matter."

"What do you live on?"

"Whatever the Lord provides. I never go hungry ... at least not very hungry."

Don asked John where he slept.

Pilgrim John smiled. "Sometimes people buy me a hotel room. I've stayed in some pretty nice places. Other times, not so nice, and once in a while in jail, but the police know me and I never break the law, so if it is in jail, it is usually just to have a warm place for the night."

"Are you Catholic?"

"I am."

"I'm Catholic too. What do priests make of you?"

"Most of them are pretty nice. I often stay at a rectory for a few days before moving on."

"Where are you staying tonight?"

John's eyes twinkled, "Probably at your house."

He was right. Don gave him a bed and a roof over his head for a few days.

Pragmatism and Pilgrimage

A few Catholic religious orders, such as the Franciscan Friars of the Renewal, still live out this form of radical discipleship. Other men and women give up everything and join enclosed contemplative communities. The hopeful news is that these radical communities are the ones that have lots of young vocations.

The radical principles of Pilgrim John are enshrined in the vows of the Franciscans: obedience, poverty, and chastity. Can "ordinary Christians" live this way? Of course we can, but in less striking ways. The way to live out the principles of obedience, poverty, and chastity is to see ourselves in this world as pilgrims or wilderness warriors.

Obedience, poverty, and chastity are the principles of "walking by faith, not by sight" (see 2 Cor. 5:7). To live by faith is to see the whole world through a different lens. Archbishop Fulton Sheen has written, "Only those who live by faith really know what is happening in the world. The great masses without faith are unconscious of the destructive processes going on, because they have lost the vision of the heights from which they have fallen."

Walking by faith through the wilderness of this world is part of what it means to be a pilgrim people. God chose a nomadic tribe for a reason. They were wanderers in the wilderness. They were dwellers in tents in a dry, thirsty land. They were poor, and their natural poverty meant they were not living self-indulgent lives of pleasure.

We can cultivate the pilgrim principles in three ways. I have already written about tithing, through which we participate in the principle of poverty. I'll go into more detail soon about the virtue of obedience, and then we'll dig into the power of chastity. For now, however, it is worth claiming the truth that we can all live out the pilgrim principles and that this is not just an option for those who follow the Lord Jesus. It is a mandate. It is not a way. It is *the* way.

13

Send My Roots Rain

Tradition and Subsidiarity versus
Progressivism and Utopianism

I'm not prone to mystical visions, but I once had an insight that
has stayed with me. In 1987, I was living in England and had
three months free between jobs, so I decided to do something
radical. I would make a hitch-hiking pilgrimage from England
to Jerusalem and stay at monasteries on the way.

At one monastery, I arrived late in the afternoon. One of the
monks ushered me in. I followed him down several corridors, then
through a doorway into the monastic cloister. The courtyard was
part of the medieval monastery. Honey-colored limestone arches
framed the walkway around the cloister. The garden itself was
simple and beautiful in its antiquity. A stone fountain burbled
in the center, and in one corner, an ancient oak spread its limbs.
At that moment, as I stepped though the door, a shaft of sun-
light illuminated the whole scene, and I had an insight about
the cloister garden.

It was a living symbol of the spiritual life. Enclosed on four
sides by the arched arcade, these four walls symbolized the Gospels. The garden was in the center—open to the sky, watered at

the very center by the fountain of life, and the tree in the cloister reached up to Heaven but only because it had deep roots. So the monastic life was enclosed from the world but open to Heaven. It was solid and alive like the ancient tree because of its deep roots of tradition.

The Hydra head of progressivism is the ideology that new is always better and we are always moving forward into a brave, new world. Progressivism dismisses tradition as dull, hidebound, legalistic, and out of date. Instead, the latest idea, the latest technology, the latest music, art, literature, scholarship, or political ideology must always be best.

Progressive Christians

As with the other Hydra heads, the venom of progressivism has poisoned and weakened the Church with one gimmick after another. Every few years, there is some new idea for evangelization, some great new idea for Church growth or for making the Church more relevant and up to date, and they all pass away like dust in the wind.

Progressives in the Church dismiss tradition as merely manmade and useless. So the gospel is updated by the shysters and hucksters of the American false gospel. Jesus came to forgive and set captives free, so the progressives turn the gospel into a social-justice campaign and turn the religion of Jesus Christ into nothing more than political activism.

Jesus came to teach us to pray and said, "the Kingdom of God is within you" (see Luke 17:21), and the New Age gurus twist His message into the search for "the God within." Jesus said to the woman guilty of adultery, "Neither do I condemn you" (John 8:11), and the progressives have turned His message into a campaign for sexual liberation and a relaxation of marriage discipline.

Jesus called us to "go into the whole world and proclaim the gospel" (Mark 16:15). The progressive thinks that is out of date and calls us simply to affirm what is beautiful, good, and true in all religions; that is enough because the latest idea is that everyone is going to be saved if they only follow "their truth" the best they can.

Tradition and Roots

Tradition is the answer to the poison of progressivism. The Sacred Scriptures teach that "no prophecy of scripture is a matter of one's own interpretation" (2 Pet. 1:20) and that we are to "test everything" (1 Thess. 5:21). Therefore, when presented with some novel teaching, doctrine, or spirituality — when presented with an innovation, religious gimmick, or bright idea — we should step back and test it against the timeless teaching of the Church.

What is tradition? It is that faith and worldview that has been handed down to us from the Apostles. The core truths of the Faith do not change with every passing age, but the expression of them can change within different cultural circumstances.

Tradition includes the doctrine and moral teachings of the Faith that are stated most clearly and in the most current form in the *Catechism of the Catholic Church*. These truths provide the roots we need to counter the false ideology of progressivism.

If progressivism is a poison in the Church, we should be aware of another Hydra head that mirrors this one. If it is not true that something is good simply because it is new, it is also not true that something is good simply because it is old. Tradition is not clinging to old-fashioned Church stuff simply *because* it is old. Being old-fashioned on purpose can be just as fake and shallow as being trendy on purpose.

Beheading Hydra

The way to avoid both the shallow trendy and the shallow traditionalist errors is to realize that tradition is not simply something published in a book. It is not an idea or a theory or a set of rules and rubrics. It is an action—a way of life. We live the tradition in the life of the Church in three ways.

First, as I've said, we live the tradition through the liturgy. In the liturgy, we are rooted in the timeless cycle of redemption. Beginning with Advent and Christmastide and moving through to Lent and Eastertide, we connect our lives with Sacred Scripture and the symbols, signs, and stories of the Faith. As we celebrate the events of salvation history, we connect our lives in a living sacramental way with the work God has been doing in the world for thousands of years, and as we do, the rhythm of worship roots our daily lives deeply in the wisdom and life of the ages.

This is one of the practical reasons for celebrating the liturgy in a solemn, reverent manner. Instead of constant innovation and striving to be relevant, we submit ourselves to the timeless heartbeat of the ancient liturgy. Instead of expressing ourselves with our own clever ideas in the liturgy, we allow ourselves to be transformed by the liturgy.

We also live the Church's tradition by learning about the lives of the saints. Pope Benedict XVI said, "Scripture can only be interpreted through the lives of the saints." The saints lived the tradition and made it real within history. As we celebrate their lives through the liturgy year by year, we come to learn about and love the saints, and as we do, we root our lives ever more deeply in the great tradition.

Finally, we send down deep roots into tradition by our moral choices. What we do with our money, what we do with our bodies, what we do with our families, our friends, and our communities all helps to consolidate and build our relationship with tradition. By living tradition in a positive, Spirit-filled way, we make tradition alive in the world, and this helps us assess the passing whims of false teachers, the ephemeral doctrines, and fashionable causes that are thrown up by progressivism.

Small Is Beautiful

This double head of the Hydra has as its foul sister the serpent of utopianism. Utopianism promises a perfect world, and that perfect world is always designed and planned by the utilitarian globalists.

Man-made utopias are ultimately totalitarian because, for the utopia to be created, it must be imposed from above. Big government always tramples the poor and the lowly. Even the socialist governments that propose to help the poor inevitably create more poverty by promoting a culture of entitlement and dependency.

The answer to globalist utopianism is the Catholic principle of subsidiarity. Subsidiarity is the idea that initiatives should be taken and solutions should be implemented at the lowest local level possible. In other words, small is beautiful and local is real.

Although a large-scale utopia is never possible, ideal communities can be created at the small, local level. I wrote a good chunk of this book at the Bethlehem Priory in California. This enclosed Norbertine community of about forty women is a good example of a mini utopia.

The sisters meet seven times a day for prayer and worship. They grow their own food; make and sell granola, incense, soaps, and perfumes; and raise Labrador puppies to earn their living. They have cows and goats for their own dairy products, and they minister to those who come to visit. They have good relations with the wider community and offer help and hospitality to those in need.

The monastic experience down through the ages is an example of subsidiarity defeating utopianism at its own game. Beginning with the first monks in Egypt in the fourth century and continuing with the blossoming of the Benedictine tradition in the Middle Ages, monasteries have shown the way of self-sufficiency, efficiency, and sound common sense. They have built real, lasting communities about as close to utopias as can be created in this world.

By building lives rooted in tradition and alive at the local level, we can build a real, concrete antidote to progressivism and utopianism. Again, this is not simply a theory or a bright idea. It is something that can be learned and applied within our daily lives.

The key principles in this case are not the Franciscan vows of obedience, chastity, and poverty, but the Benedictine vows of obedience, stability, and conversion of life.[53] Obedience breaks the curse of individualism, stability is a commitment to putting down deep roots, and conversion of life is the total transformation of the individual by God's grace.

Is it possible to pursue this radical way of life in our high-tech, busy world? I believe it is, but to do so, we must envision our parish communities as the locations for this alternative. The parish is composed of households, and each household can become a place of tradition, prayer, and action in the world. Then, as members of households come together for worship, education, and care for one another, the building blocks are put in place for outreach to the wider community in evangelization and social service.[54]

---

[53] See Dwight Longenecker, *Listen My Son: St Benedict for Fathers* (Harrisburg, PA: Morehouse, 2002).

[54] Rod Dreher's book *The Benedict Option* goes into detail on the history and theory of the monastic example of building local,

Working at this local level, the poison of progressivism and the false dream of utopianism can be defeated, not with argument, debate, or discussion but through real action by real people who are simply rolling up their sleeves and doing what they can where they are and with what they have.

---

creatively subversive communities. Leah Libresco's *Building the Benedict Option* is a practical guide to doing so.

14

Just As I Am

Relativism and Indifferentism versus Truth and Authority

If there's one chapter of this book I feel is really essential, this is it. Although it comes toward the end of the book, this chapter is, in many ways, the most important, because here I will explain the most basic solutions to the core problem. Here I will explain not only how to behead some of the Hydra heads but how to slay the old dragon in your own life.

It's easy to think that relativism is a modern problem. In fact, it is as old as Pontius Pilate. You'll remember that Pontius Pilate interviewed Jesus and asked, "What is truth?" (John 18:38). Pilate had good reason to ask such a question because the world of the Roman Empire was just as much awash with different ideas about truth as the modern world is. Because of travel and trade, the Roman Empire was flooded with a smorgasbord of religions, philosophies, and ideologies. The ancient paganism of the Middle East jockeyed with the religious thought and practices of Africa, Asia, and Europe. Greek philosophy, Roman political ideas, and myths swirled through society. Everywhere you went, festivals, sacrifices, and rituals were taking place in shrines and temples built to honor a huge array of gods and goddesses.

Pilate's cynical question is the same question that echoes through our modern society today: "What is truth?"

It is easy enough for Catholics of a certain stripe to step up at this point and pull out their apologetics weaponry to make arguments for the existence of God and for the truth of the Catholic religion. I'm not opposed to such exercises, and I believe energetic apologetics generally do a lot of good.

Remembering, however, that the two worldviews (atheistic materialism and religious belief) are so fundamentally contradictory, I think apologetics efforts will now have limited success. Instead, I'd like to be more creatively subversive and suggest that the way to decapitate the Hydra head of relativism is to revisit that scene in which Jesus stood before Pilate.

Pilate asks, "What is truth?" The Man who said, "I am the way and the truth and the life" (John 14:6) stood before him. Note that Jesus did not say, "I teach the truth" or "I can point you to the truth" or even "I speak the truth" or "I *do* the truth." He said, "I *am* the truth." In doing so, He was affirming something far more astonishing than any other religious teacher would claim. He was asserting that His whole existence — who He *is* — is truth.

In fact, He was asserting something even more surprising. In using the words "I AM," He was uttering the sacred name of God that was revealed to Moses at the burning bush. When Moses asked God what His name was, God said, "I AM" (see Exod. 3:14). In other words, God does not simply exist. He is the source of existence. He is life. He is existence itself. So when Jesus said, "I AM," He was making a claim so astounding that it must be faced.

With this claim, Jesus of Nazareth places Himself outside the category of all the other founders of religion, spiritual teachers, philosophers, and saints. Either He is God incarnate, as He claims, or, as C. S. Lewis has argued, He is a fraud of the highest degree or a madman. I will not put forward pages of arguments on this point. There are plenty of better thinkers and writers who have done so. If you are interested, go look them up. Instead, I would challenge you to confront the person, not the argument.

This is the answer to Pilate's question and to modern relativism; it is your answer and my answer: the answer is not arguments for the existence of God and theological arguments for the truth of the Catholic Faith. The answer is a personal encounter with Jesus Christ—who is truth.

Billy Graham Lives

A few years ago, I was traveling down Interstate 85 from North Carolina to our home in South Carolina. As I traveled south toward Charlotte, I noticed that the northbound side of the highway was closed. As I approached Charlotte, the bridges over the highway were crowded with emergency vehicles with their lights blazing. The farther south I went, the more the bridges were packed with cars and trucks. Then I saw people standing by the side of the highway.

Eventually I saw motorcycle outriders coming up the northbound highway. They were followed by a funeral cortege. Then I remembered. The evangelist Billy Graham had died. I was witnessing the transfer of his body from Charlotte to Washington, DC, where it was to lie in state in the capital. Suddenly I was choked up. This was amazing! No news channels covered it. It was not on social media, but thousands of people turned up along the highway to pay their respects to the famous evangelist. I had never seen anything like it.

That night, I went home and watched an old Billy Graham rally on YouTube. Graham spoke simply and powerfully to the crowd of thousands packed into a baseball stadium. He didn't argue about the existence of God. He didn't discuss in detail the sixteen deadly isms in our society. He simply spoke about our separation from God by sin and Christ's death on the Cross to pay the price of our reconciliation with Him. Then he invited people to get up out of their seats and come forward to give their lives to Christ, who had given His life for them.

And they did. Thousands got up and went forward. Watching this reminded me that, at the base of it all, the truth of the world is Jesus Christ, and to know Him and the power of His Cross is to know the truth not only with our heads but with our hearts and souls and our whole being.

It pains me to write for a largely Catholic audience and to have to assert this basic, underlying, bottom-line reality: The Christian faith is *not* primarily about rules and regulations for respectable people. It is not about being good enough to make it into Heaven. It is not about trying very hard to be nice and kind to other people. It is not even about going to church, saying our prayers, and trying very hard to believe things that in our worst moments we suspect might be a lot of hogwash. It is not even first and foremost about being a 100 percent, signed-up, living-in-a-state-of-grace, going-to-Mass-every-week, and saying-the-Rosary-every-day kind of Catholic.

Don't misunderstand me. These things are good as far as they go, but there is more to it than this.

You Must Be Born Again

The Christian faith is about a firsthand, heartfelt, life-changing, soul-wrenching, eye-opening, lip-trembling, spine-chilling, face-to-face encounter with the Lord Jesus Christ, King of the Universe, Son of God and Son of Mary, the Lamb of God who

takes away the sins of the world. It is about falling at the foot
of the Cross where He laid down His life and knowing that the
blood from His side has washed away your sin and turned your
life around and that you will never be the same again.

This is truth. The truth is an experience and an existence.
The truth is standing before the burning bush and hearing the
voice rumble deep and low, "I AM" and then slipping off your
shoes because you are on holy ground, falling on your face, and
acknowledging the I AM by whispering "And here *I* am. Just as
I am."

> Just as I am, without one plea,
> But that Thy blood was shed for me,
> And that Thou bid'st me come to Thee,
> O Lamb of God, I come![55]

The truth is being brought to the realization that this is the
most important thing in the world, and in the face of this Person
who is truth, everything else is secondary. This is what the philosophers and scoffers have hated and spat upon. It is this simple
realization and repentance that they either did not, could not,
or would not understand and accept.

I will speak from the heart. Coming home from Sunday-night
church one evening when I was five years old, I told my mother
I wanted to "get saved." She knelt and led me in this simple but
world-changing action. I said I was sorry for my sins and I wanted
to accept Jesus Christ as my Lord and Savior. I am not ashamed
of this. I will tell anyone who has ears to hear. Even though I
am a Catholic priest, I still tell people that this simple action of
being "born again" is the most important thing.

[55]   Charlotte Elliott, "Just as I Am" (1835).

I believe more than this. I believe the glorious fullness of the historical Catholic faith. I believe the sacraments are real and necessary, but personal faith—whenever and however it comes to us—is also real and necessary. This is what the Catholic religion is about, and if you have not grasped this yet, reach out and get ahold of it now before it is too late.

I will take a moment now and ask you: Have you ever come to this point? Have you ever come to this encounter with the One who is truth and fallen on your knees in His awesome presence and said with all your heart, soul, mind, and strength, "Lord Jesus Christ, Son of the living God, have mercy on me, a sinner?"

If you were baptized as an infant, then the grace you received on that day is meant to bring you to this encounter. If you were confirmed at fourteen, the grace you received then helped to bring you to this encounter. Every time you go to Confession or go to Mass, you have the opportunity to come to this encounter. The sacraments are not something different from this encounter. They are the formal and objective aspect of this encounter.

If you want to destroy relativism in your life—if you want to behead the Hydra, then do this right now. Stop reading this book and open your heart to the Lord Jesus Christ and say the simplest and most beautiful prayer of all. Say to the Lord Jesus Christ, "Have mercy on me, a sinner. Come and meet me. I am Yours. I want to be in You and You to be in me. I do not simply want to acknowledge the truth in my mind by believing certain things. I do not wish any longer simply to follow a religion of rules and regulations. I wish to encounter You and to be filled with Your Holy Spirit so that I might live and dwell and be one with the Truth."

To confess our sins and accept Christ's forgiveness is the ba-sic transaction we enter into when we come to Mass or go to

Confession, but too many Catholics go through those routines and it never hits them between the eyes that these experiences, too, are one of the ways to encounter Christ—to repent of our sins, accept Jesus, and be born again.

Let me say, however, that I am not referring to merely a subjective, emotional conversion experience. If the encounter with Christ is authentic, it will be validated by the objective sacrament of Baptism and evidenced in a changed life. Those who have had the encounter will rise from the quicksand of modern relativism. They will have a new direction, a new vision, and a new purpose in life. They will begin to know in the depths of their being that they have imbibed God Himself.

They have sipped eternity and embraced the one who is the way, the truth, and the life and have been infused with His Spirit. Relativism will evaporate in the heat of this experience as newborn believers begin to live lives of genuine reality and concrete purpose. In this new light, relativism will fade like the darkness at dawn.

Truth Revealed and Made Real

This personal experience is vitally important, but on its own, it leads to the Hydra head of indifference. If the Faith is *only* about the personal experience, then the person who says, "All that really matters is how much we love Jesus" is correct.

This is only one step away from saying, "Jewish, Buddhist, Seventh-Day Adventist, Hindu, Shintoist, or pagan: all that really matters is that we are sincere." The personal experience needs to be grounded in the objective sacraments of the Church, but it also needs to be rooted in an objective authority structure that transcends our own personal experience.

Jesus Christ is the truth, but He established His Church to preach the truth of who He really is and to interpret and apply the truth to the real circumstances of life. The Catholic Church offers that authority, and there are twelve traits—in six paired sets—that show how comprehensive and complete the Catholic claims of authority are.

To examine them, we might ask, "What kind of authority might a group of Christians who were deliberating a difficult matter need to assist them in their decision?"

It is rooted in history . . .

First of all, their decision would have to be made from a historical perspective. It would not be good enough to decide complex moral, social, or doctrinal issues based on popularity polls or yesterday's newspaper.

In addition, the authority has to show a real continuity with the historical experience of Christianity. The Protestant churches that have existed for four or five hundred years can demonstrate this to a degree, but only the Catholic and Eastern Orthodox churches have a living link that goes back to Roman times—and, through Judaism, back to the beginning of human history.

. . . but up to date

The historical link is essential, but, on its own, it is not sufficient. Historical authority has to be balanced with the ability to be applied in the present day to present concerns. An authority that is only historical becomes ossified. An authority that cannot be applied to contemporary issues is not just rooted in history; it is bound by history.

It is objective . . .

A third quality of a valid authority system is that it needs to be objective. By this, I mean it needs to be independent of any one person's or group's agenda, ideology, philosophy, or self-interest. A valid authority transcends all political, economic, and cultural pressures.

. . . but flexible

For the authority to be valid, however, it cannot rely on abstract principles and objective criteria alone. In other words, it understands the complexities of real life and the pastoral exigencies of helping real people.

It is universal . . .

An authority can speak to all situations only if it comes from a universal source. This source of authority needs to be universal not only geographically but also chronologically. In other words, it transcends national agendas and limitations, but it also transcends the cultural trends and intellectual fashions of any particular time.

. . . but local

However, this universal authority needs to be applied in a particular, local way. An authority that is only universal remains vague, abstract, and disincarnate — that is, without any physical grounding. For a universal authority system to be valid, it also must be expressed locally. Catholicism speaks with a universal voice, but it is also as local as St. Patrick's Church and Fr. Magee on the corner of Chestnut Street.

It is intellectually challenging . . .

If an authority system is to speak to the complexities of the human situation, it must be able to hold its own with the philosophical and intellectual experts in every field of human endeavor. This

authority must not only be able to contend with the intellectual experts in all fields but must be intellectually satisfying and
coherent within itself.

. . . but accessible to the uneducated

Nonetheless, while the authority system must be intellectually
top-notch, the religious system must also be accessible to ordinary people — even the illiterate. A religious system that is only
intellectual can speak only for the learned.

It is invisible . . .

The Church is made up of all people everywhere who trust in
Christ and are baptized. Identifying this group is impossible because we do not know every heart and every soul. Therefore, the
true Church is invisible.

. . . but visible

This characteristic alone is not satisfactory, however, because human beings locked in the visible plane of reality also demand that
the Church be visible. The Catholic system of authority recognizes
both the invisible dimension of the Church and the visible.

It is both human and divine

Finally, in order to speak with authority, the Church must be
both human and divine. An authority that speaks only with
a divine voice lacks the authenticity that comes with human
experience. So Islam and Mormonism, which are both based on
books supposedly dictated by angels, are unsatisfactory because
their authority is supernaturally imposed on the human condition.

On the other hand, a religion that is purely a construct of
the human condition is merely a system of good works, religious

techniques, or good ideas. Christian Science and Unitarianism, for example, were developed only from human understandings and natural goodness. As such, both lack a supernatural voice of authority.

Built upon the Rock

Some churches may exercise some of the twelve traits, but only the Catholic Church is able to field all twelve as a foundation for decision-making.

This authority works infallibly through the active ministry of the whole Church. The *Catechism of the Catholic Church* says that it is Christ who is infallible, and He grants a measure of His infallibility to His Body, the Church. That infallibility is worked out through these twelve traits, but it is expressed most majestically and fully through Christ's minister of infallibility: one person — the Rock on which the Church is built, Peter and his successors.

It is this personal, life-changing encounter with the One who is truth, deepened and rooted in the authority of the Church, that is the rock on which Western civilization was founded. As Jesus taught us, "Everyone who listens to these words of mine and acts on them will be like a wise man who built his house on rock. The rain fell, the floods came, and the winds blew and buffeted the house. But it did not collapse; it had been set solidly on rock. And everyone who listens to these words of mine but does not act on them will be like a fool who built his house on sand. The rain fell, the floods came, and the winds blew and buffeted the house. And it collapsed and was completely ruined" (see Matt. 7:24–27).

15

There's No Other Way

Obedience and Community versus
Individualism and Tribalism

In my Sunday-school days, we sang a simple chorus I cannot forget. It went like this: "Trust and obey, for there's no other way, to be happy in Jesus, than to trust and obey." My dad used to sing it as we were getting ready for church, and I should add that he sang it at the top of his voice, and we kids rolled our eyes, knowing that it was a trite kiddy song, but with a tinge of irony, knowing also that "unless you turn and become like children, you will not enter the kingdom of heaven" (Matt. 18:3).

Regarding radical discipleship and being a creative subversive, there are few things more subversive and radical in the modern world than the concept of trustful obedience. The entire worldly culture is founded on the idea of total and absolute individualism—what Carl Trueman calls "expressive individualism"—the notion that because there is no greater meaning or purpose in the world, it is up to me and Frank Sinatra to "do it my way."

"Obedience! Not for me!" the modern Western person says. "And not just 'not me' because I'm a rebellious brat, but because there is no greater authority in Heaven or earth to whom my obedience is due. It's my body. My choice. Right? There is no one to trust and no one to obey, so I not only may do as I please; I *must* do as I please."

We saw in chapter 6, however, how individuals can eventually join a tribe that destroys their individualism. Obedience is the paradoxical principle that stands this whole problem on its head. St. Benedict and all the great spiritual masters say that it is in obedience that we find true freedom. How so?

There is a deeper meaning to the virtue of obedience that is locked into the root meaning of the word. The word *obedience* comes from the word Latin *oboedire*, which means "to listen" or "to pay attention." Indeed, the first word of St. Benedict's Rule is *Listen*. To obey is to listen, to be alert, to be discerning and attentive to the voice of the Lord.

Metanoia Mentality

This shift from "my way" to "Thy way" begins with the most fundamental and radical action of all: repentance. The word in the original Greek Scriptures for repentance is *metanoia*, which means "changing one's mind." This sounds rather shallow, like changing your order at the restaurant, but the real meaning is much more powerful. It means a total, deep transformation of one's perspective. It means a completely different mindset and understanding of oneself and one's place in the world. It means looking toward Heaven instead of looking toward earth. It is shifting the energy and life to God's kingdom.

Furthermore, this repentance is not a once-and-done action. It is a continuing attitude and action. The metanoia mentality is to be constantly aware of the need to turn again away from me, myself, and I and to turn to God's way. True repentance, therefore, lays the foundation for the radical call to obedience that severs the head of proud individualism.

Repentance is the brilliant first step in following Christ. Right there at the beginning, we say, "I am not right all the time. I have got things wrong. If sin is falling short of the glory of God, then I have sinned big time, and I want to live differently. I want to trust and obey."

Almighty Me

The truth is that "we are not some casual and meaningless product of evolution. Each of us is the result of a thought of God. Each of us is willed, each of us is loved, each of us is necessary."[56] When we say to God, "Thy will be done," we are prodigals returning to the Father's house. When we say "Thy will be done," we join forces with the One who created us. Because we are created in God's image and likeness, we share in His attributes. One of His attributes is omnipotence. He is all powerful. Therefore, if we are created in His image, it follows that we too are powerful (in a much diminished way). We have free will. We really can make choices. We really can change the world, change history, and change our lives.

We have this quality called "will," which is our small share in omnipotence. As long as we exercise this in a totally individualistic way, we are abusing that will and making ourselves into little gods and goddesses. But when we yield our will to God and say, "Thy will be done," we plug our will into the power from which it came. When we say "Thy will be done," we join our will with God's, and, as the Lord Jesus says, "for God all things are possible" (Matt. 19:26).

---

[56] Pope Benedict XVI, inaugural homily.

Furthermore, it is in conforming our will to God's that we achieve true freedom. Why? Because God's will for us is to become who He created us to be. He created us to be happy, to live in harmony with Him and with one another and with His created order. He created us to be fulfilled and to grow into the full stature of our human potential (see Eph. 4:13). To become this kind of person is to be truly empowered, happy, fulfilled, and free.

As in the other chapters of this second part of this book, this method of decapitating a head of the Hydra is not a theory or an idea. It is real. It is practical. Obedience is not an attitude. It is an action. Individualism is defeated not by argument or debate but by rolling up our sleeves and getting on with the job.

Whom Should I Obey?

While it is natural to kick against the idea of obedience, it is easy to overlook the fact that all of us have to live within certain structures of obedience every day. Every day we obey the laws of nature, the laws of life, and the laws of decent moral behavior. Every day we live a life obedient to certain rituals, routines, rules, and regulations. When you stop to think about it, obedience is not so unusual. In fact, obedience is the default setting. What is strange is the modern assumption that obedience is somehow unnatural, disordered, and shocking.

Toward the end of his Rule, St. Benedict says the monks should all obey one another. In other words, their life of obedience culminates in an attitude of obedience, and if *obedience* means "listening," then to obey one another means to listen carefully to the needs and concerns of others. Obedience, therefore, is a lifestyle of listening and being sensitive to others and of seeking to serve them in love.

This is the true source of our work with the poor, the lonely, prisoners, the sick, and the needy. We care for them not out of some politically correct social justice agenda but because they are our brothers and sisters and because we live in an attitude of obedience — listening to and serving others in humble obedience.

Who Am I?

One of the major problems in the modern, fragmented, individualistic world concerns genuine human identity. For all the complicated reasons we have discussed, individuals don't know who they are, what their purpose is, and where they belong.

But Carl Trueman points out that our identity is determined by our community. We are recognized by our circle of family, friends, work colleagues, and the wider world. Our identity is not only recognized but also formed by the community. Trueman quotes the philosopher Charles Taylor: "One is a self only among other selves. A self can never be described without reference to those who surround it."[57]

As the poet John Donne has written, "No man is an island, entire of itself." Part of the alienation of modern man is the fact that the community of the extended family, ethnic and national identity, local identity, and religious identity has been broken, and the false ideology of individualism contributes to this terrible alienation.

Furthermore, Rousseau and Freud bequeathed to the modern world the idea that it was society (and especially religion) that acted to restrict our personal freedom. Instead of helping to form our identity, Rousseau and Freud argued, our relationships and society are the enemy of our desires and our "true selves." This

[57] Trueman, *The Rise and Triumph*, 57.

idea has contributed to the anger, suspicion, and resentment toward all establishment authority systems and is the reason the sense of authority has disintegrated in our Western world.

This is why tribalism is so powerful a force in our society. Alienated individuals are desperate not only to belong but also to have their identity recognized and affirmed. The tribe offers an alternative structure of belonging. The tribe seduces the lonely individual with the promise of community — not a community that affirms them and forms them, but a kind of anti-community — a tribe of howling rebels.

The tribe is the ape of true community. The tribe is no more than a mob extension of the individualist, and, as such, it seeks to impose on others the values, identity, and agenda of the tribe. The tribe, like the individualist, is self-identifying, self-serving, and self-centered. The tribe, like the individualist, is aggressive and assertive. The tribe, like the individualist, considers other tribes to be a threat. The tribe, like the individualist, is always restless, unsatisfied, primed, and ready for war.

Tribalism is one of the ugliest heads of the Hydra and one of the most difficult to get rid of because the tribe, like the individualist, is self-righteous and proud. The group dynamic of the tribe feeds that self-righteousness and magnifies that pride.

Community and Communion

The antidote to tribalism is community. This is tricky because, at first, Christian community might seem to resemble tribalism, and an unhealthy Christian community can certainly be a manifestation of tribalism. True Christian community, however, is built not on envy and rage but on grace, charity, and mutual service.

Christian community is the family of God, united in Christ Jesus, whom each individual has encountered. Through personal

conversion and the Church's Sacraments of Initiation, each individual is bonded with Christ and becomes a cell in His Body.
The authentic Christian community, therefore, is a mystical
living organism — not a tribe.

This living organism, which is the Body of Christ, is also
distinguished from the tribe in what it does. The tribe is self-identifying, self-serving, and self-centered. The Body of Christ — the
Christian community — does in the world today what Jesus Christ
did when He was here. When Jesus Christ was on earth, He did
five main things: (1) He taught the truth; (2) He healed the sick;
(3) He forgave sins; (4) He asserted authority over evil; and (5)
He gave Himself for the world's redemption. This is the work
of true Christian community, and as the community does this
work, it defeats the activism, envy, rage, and violence of the tribe.

Where and how do we build such community? First, we establish community in the home. Husband, wife, and children are the
first building blocks of a community. Notice how, in the establishment of the primary community of the family, the tendency to
individualism is immediately beheaded. When you marry someone,
you must lay individual selfish concerns aside. You no longer live
for yourself. You live for your spouse and your children. This is
what marriage is: the destruction of individualism by the spouses'
obedience to each other and the destruction of tribalism by the
establishment of a community of love and service rather than envy.

The second level of community is the parish. The parish is
an extended family. All members of the parish are brothers and
sisters because they share the same bloodline — the bloodline of
Jesus Christ the King.

One of the great problems in the Church today is that too
many American Catholics are not willing to invest in the community of the family or the community of the parish. Instead, they

treat their church like a franchise operation. The local church is where they go to consume religion on their own terms, in their own time, and they expect good customer service!

Instead of this, join a parish community. Get involved. Volunteer. Support the parish with your tithe. Build the community of the parish and destroy tribalism with genuine service, prayer, and concern for others.

The third level of community is the diocese, and the fourth is the global church. In a world of religious indifferentism and an ever-increasing number of denominations and religions, the Catholic Church is the one community that really is global and provides a worldwide community of brothers and sisters.

Finally, obedience and community come together in the Church when we attempt to live within the authority and teaching of the Church in our everyday lives. By simply living out our Faith to the best of our abilities, we live by a different standard. We build our houses on rock, not on shifting sands, and as we do, we banish the antichrists, obliterate the prince of this world, and behead the Hydra.

16

Learning and Loving

*Education and Charity versus
Sentimentalism and Romanticism*

If you've ever worked with someone who suffers from addiction, you'll know how difficult it is to get through to that person. Most people with addictions have developed a complex maze of lies under which they duck for cover. They use others to hide behind and play on their concerns. They manipulate and use emotional blackmail and will do most anything to maintain their addiction. Worst of all, they behave in this way unconsciously and instinctively. They live a lie while pretending there is no problem.

Sentimentalists are like this. They are addicted to their own niceness. Being nice makes them feel good. It gives them a buzz. They feel good not only about the object of their kindly feelings but also about themselves for having those kindly feelings. And as with any drug that makes you feel good, they want to go back for more.

How does one battle sentimentalism? Once again, a direct attack doesn't work. As addicts deny their addictions and become angry, so sentimentalists get angry if their sentimentality is questioned. If one either does not share the sentiment or suggests that the feelings are misplaced or disordered, the niceness soon evaporates either into anger and blame or self-pity. If it is anger, then sentimentalists attack, blaming their critics for being hard-hearted, cruel, or even wicked. If the response is self-pity, sentimentalists lapse into victim mode. In both cases — anger and self-pity — sentimentalists indulge in yet another round of emotion and use the emotion to manipulate others. Like addicts, they wallow in their addiction and use it to control others.

As with any addiction, whatever the emotional response is, it continues to multiply within the personality. The further problem with sentimentalism is that it is usually linked, like the Hydra heads, with other isms. Sentimentality amplifies the tendency to utilitarianism and individualism. It bundles emotion into tribalism and romanticism, heightening their power in the person's life.

Sentimentalism also can't be attacked head-on because sentimentalists are unaware that they are sentimentalists. They are already operating under the assumption that their emotions are the only criteria for judgment and are blind to the thought that there might be some transcendent, objective criteria for truth beyond their own feelings.

The radical answer to sentimentality is education. Down through history, one of the strengths of every creatively subversive movement has been to establish schools. A proper education corrects sentimentalism with objective learning. The right kind of education is not simply the accumulation of facts or vocational training but is also a formation in thinking that helps to order the emotions properly.

In saying that education is the answer to sentimentality, however, I should add that contemporary secular education does not correct sentimentality. Why? Because the philosophies we discussed in the first part of this book are the foundation of modern educational theory. Although American schools, colleges, and universities would shy away from the "atheist" label, they are, in fact, institutions of atheist propaganda.

The greater number of our teachers and administrators in secular educational establishments teach their subjects through the lens of the sixteen isms. Religion is proscribed. Materialism, scientism, and historicism are the dogmas. Utilitarianism, pragmatism, and progressivism are the unquestioned assumptions. Individualism, sentimentalism, and Freudianism are the air they breathe. Eroticism, romanticism, and tribalism are the parameters of their lifestyle. Not only do they indoctrinate their students in this propaganda, but they themselves have been educated in this worldview from the start.

Education in modern American schools and colleges, therefore, does not help to correct sentimentalism but confirms and promotes it as well as the other heads of the Hydra. It would also be a mistake to imagine that this is simply the curriculum at the college level. It is the underlying philosophy of education and the worldview of the whole secular education system.

A Classical Education

Therefore, to take a radical position against sentimentalism, one must look elsewhere for the right kind of education. It is all well and good to homeschool our children or establish a Catholic parish or Christian school, but unless the curriculum and philosophy of education are carefully thought through and developed, the danger is that all we do is add a few prayers and Bible readings to an education that has atheistic materialism as its foundation. When we do this, we are actually baptizing and condoning the atheistic propaganda!

There is not room in this book to go into detail explaining classical education. The Association of Classical and Christian Schools and the Institute for Catholic Liberal Education are two organizations committed to the support and expansion of classical education.

Very briefly, a classical education not only teaches facts but also teaches children how to think, analyze, and process their learning. Teaching is usually done by the Socratic method — the teacher asking questions to promote discussion and direct the enquiring mind. Instead of breaking the day into fragments of learning in separate subject areas, classical education utilizes cross-curricular teaching. One instructor may teach philosophy, geography, literature, theology, and history all in one unit. So, for example, the Bible stories of the New Testament will be taught alongside the geography and politics of the ancient Middle East, the philosophy and theology of the first century, and the secular literature of the age. In this way, the student makes connections and has the tools to process and analyze his learning.

Most classical schools employ a structure of three stages of learning that are linked to child development. Grammar is the first, and this includes reading, writing, and the fundamentals of each subject. Logic is the process of correct reasoning, and rhetoric uses the skills of logic to help the student analyze, debate, and process the learning.

In this way, critical skills are developed, the mind is honed, and the personality is formed in an educational method that is deeply traditional and profound. When this takes place within a strongly Christian environment through a church school or a home school, not only sentimentalism but all of the isms are understood for what they are, where they originated, how they are connected, and how they can be countered.

Finally, a classical education is often taught according to a "chronological spine." In our parish school, the students follow a twelve-year plan split into three groups of four historical periods. In first grade, the children study the ancient world: the Old Testament period. In second grade, they study the New Testament world: the Roman Empire and beyond. In third grade, they study the medieval period, and in fourth grade, the period of the last five hundred years. Most of their studies are viewed through the lens of that year's epoch. In grades five through eight, they repeat those time periods but in more depth, and in grades nine through twelve, they repeat them again—this time studying the great books in their original languages. As a result, our students graduating from twelfth grade understand the modern world, understand the heads of the Hydra, and have both the knowledge and the intellectual skills to live an informed, sensitive, intelligent, and committed Catholic life.

Sentimentalism doesn't have a chance!

The Four Loves

The other Hydra head associated with sentimentalism—romanticism—doesn't have a chance either. Romanticism is sentimentalism on steroids. It is the elevation of individual emotion to the exclusion of all other forms of knowledge or authority. Romanticism treats the individual emotions as a kind of divine revelation, and those emotions are invariably some exalted form of love—love of self, love of nature, love of beauty, love of the ideal lover, love of pleasure, love of wealth.

But romanticism is a distorted love. It is a love of self and a love of one's emotions projected on the whole world and the lens through which the entire world is viewed. The remedy for romanticism is to correct that love and redirect it according to proper priorities.

In his book *The Four Loves*, C. S. Lewis outlines the different forms of love. He puts the love of the material world on one side and looks at the love we have for others. He takes the names for the four loves from four Greek words. *Storge* is family affection — the natural love that flows from being needed and needing others. *Philia* is friendship love — the love that people share while enjoying a mutual pastime or pleasure. *Eros* is romantic, erotic love, and *agape* is unconditional love — desiring only the good of the other person.

Romanticism, through its intrinsic self-centeredness, twists and destroys all four forms of love. It sees *storge* as a burden and a restriction. The mundane duties of family life are dismissed with self-dramatized hauteur. *Philia* is twisted by being intertwined with eros. The romantic person may drift into decadence and fall into sexual relationships with people who are properly only friends. *Eros* is twisted into promiscuity and hyper-dramatized, sentimental relationships, and *agape* (objective, disinterested love) is simply incomprehensible for the person caught up in romanticism.

Lewis's structure of the four loves, therefore, corrects the excesses of romanticism, and since creative subversion is not just theoretical but active, it is within the creation of positive, family-based, local communities that these four loves find proper and wholesome expression. Within the family, *storge* and *eros* are expressed, fulfilled, and put into action. Within the school and parish, *philia* is learned and practiced, and within the liturgy and social action in the wider community, *agape* — unconditional love of God and neighbor — can be realized in a positive, radiant, and powerful way.

By investing in solid, Catholic, classical education, we sever the head of subjective sentimentalism. By building proper, balanced relationships with family, friends, spouses, and God and our neighbor, we correct the heightened individual sentimentalism of romanticism. Such practical action and solid achievement at the down-to-earth level of family, parish, and school is long-lasting, beautiful, and true. It builds a strong foundation in hearts and homes for a hopeful future.

17

Knowing Me, Knowing You

Marriage and Chastity versus Eroticism and Freudianism

A maxim from ancient Greece advised "Know thyself," and the Greek philosopher Socrates observed, "The unexamined life is not worth living." I can remember an old preacher pointing out that in the book of Genesis, the quaint old King James Version of the Bible said, "Adam knew Eve his wife" (4:1). That's profound, eloquent, and dignified. Modern versions are curiously coy: "Adam had relations with his wife Eve" or "Adam made love to his wife Eve."

The older version is not only quainter and more dignified; it also communicates the original Hebrew better. Hebrew, like most ancient languages, has a small vocabulary. Therefore, one word carries multiple levels of meaning. The word translated as "know," which is being used for sexual intercourse, is *yada*, which is also used in Exodus in a command to "know" the Lord God and elsewhere in the Old Testament for the intimate encounter with God's glory (Hab. 2:14). Elsewhere, the same word means "to reveal." The ancient wisdom of Genesis, therefore, means that in the sexual act, more is going on than just playful mutual titillation ending in a spasm of pleasure.

Beheading Hydra

The word *Genesis* means "at the beginning," and the story of Adam and Eve is about sin and sex. It is therefore about human beginnings. It is also about the beginning, or foundation, of all things, including the foundational truths of human identity. It teaches us that the sexual act is intrinsically tied up with knowing who we are and knowing one another. When we make love, we get naked, and in doing so we reveal not only our bodies but ourselves. We get to know one another in the most intimate way by entering one another's bodies, and because bodies and souls are one, we also enter the other person's psyche, soul, and identity.

So, through the sexual act, Adam knew Eve and Eve knew Adam. And in knowing Eve, Adam came to know himself; and in knowing Adam, Eve came to know herself. In giving themselves to each other, they knew the other person and so came to know themselves.

From this profound story of humanity's origins, we conclude that I can know myself only in relationship to other people. Think about it. The completely isolated individual, the expressive individualist, has no point of reference by which to know himself. He has only his inner psychology, which, the longer he studies it, becomes ever more mysterious and elusive. He can know himself only in reference to his inner desires, thoughts, intentions, and motivations, and they are a complex network of constantly shifting, interwoven connections.

There is no way, therefore, that he can validate his experience. Does he really know himself? How can he know? How does he know whether what he thinks he is, is, in fact, an illusion of pride and self-love or self-hatred and doubt? There is no way he can find approval and recognition because approving of oneself and recognizing oneself is an inward spiral—a contradiction of the whole idea of approval and recognition.

In other words, we can know ourselves only as others come to know us. Other ways of trying to know ourselves are invariably self-referential and narcissistic. It can never be more than gazing at ourselves in a mirror. Looking within, without any external point of reference, is like being lost in a house of mirrors.

This is why love is important: because when we love another person, we have an external point of reference by which to know ourselves. This is why prayer is important: in prayer and worship we also have an external point of reference by which we can test ourselves and therefore come to know ourselves. Without such external points of reference, we are dancing with shadows of ourselves.

Promise and Promiscuity

This is the promise of love: that we might come to be known as we are known (see 1 Cor. 13:12). Love promises us mutual recognition and approval and, with that mutual recognition and approval, mutual self-knowledge and maturity. If the unexamined life is not worth living, we should examine life through love and discover that it is indeed worth living.

This kind of self-examination, self-knowledge, and personal growth requires trust. We're tough. We're crustaceans. We have exoskeletons. It's difficult to be vulnerable and to let someone else into our lives, but this is precisely the promise of love: someone else is going to get inside us and get to know us. This kind of relationship requires total, unconditional trust between two people. It requires a covenant, a deal, an unbreakable bond if this mutual self-examination and knowledge is to take place.

Furthermore, to examine life thoroughly — to examine oneself completely — takes not only trust but also time. I need to get used to that other person. I need to make sure my trust was not misplaced. Furthermore, I need to grow with and examine life with that other person. In order to know that person and know myself, we need to go through life's joys and sorrows together. In fact, this process does not just take time: it takes a lifetime.

This is why marriage is supposed to be an unbreakable bond that lasts until "death do us part." The bond of trust on which marriage is grounded is fragile and easily broken, and when it breaks, people are hurt. Wives are hurt. Husbands are hurt. Children are hurt. Families are hurt. The Church is hurt. Society is hurt. Furthermore, every time that bond of trust is broken, we grow another shell to protect ourselves. The one-night stand, the shallow, short-term love affair, the betrayal of adultery, and the harsh divorce not only hurt people; they also harden hearts and make real love difficult.

Christians are opposed to things that hurt people. Therefore, Christians have always been opposed to the things that break the beautiful, fragile bond of marriage. We all know the long list: adultery, promiscuity, prostitution, rape, child sex abuse, masturbation, pornography, homosexuality, divorce, and remarriage. All these actions break marriage and therefore hinder us from truly knowing ourselves and knowing others.

Masturbation and Immaturity

Someone once commented about an immature young man's sexual habits, "Poor George. He has no one to love him, so he has to love himself." That compassionate comment exposes the entire agenda of the erotic society. Individualism turns the center of the universe inward to me, myself, and I. Sentimentalism and romanticism make my inner emotions the standard of all things. I become my own judge. Eroticism makes my sexual feelings and instincts the standard of happiness. Freudianism says those feelings are merely healthy instincts that should be acted on. In other words, my own happiness is based not just on what I feel but on *who* I feel. "Making love"—in fact the whole meaning of life itself—becomes no more than the quest to find genital contentment.

Eroticism and Freudianism not only encourage promiscuity; they produce the current widespread assumption that unrestrained sexual expression is natural and good and that any restriction of sexual activity must be repressive and bad.

Given the strength of the human libido, the erotic society must end up being a promiscuous society, and if, through the technology of contraceptives and abortion, procreation is avoided, this promiscuous society must, in fact, be a masturbatory society, for what is the enjoyment of sexual pleasure without real commitment and openness to the gift of children except various forms of masturbation?

The expression of sexuality always reflects the philosophy of the culture. In a fecund, mature, loving society, marriage and procreation will be the expression. In an immature, adolescent, spoiled, individualistic society, masturbation will be the expression. It follows: individualism is self-love. Masturbation is the sexual expression of that narcissistic mentality.

"Poor George. He has no one to love him, so he has to love himself." This is the sadness of sexual sin: George will never really examine life as long as he continues only to examine his genitals. Furthermore, even when he does enter into a sexual relationship, in a narcissistic society, those relationships will rarely rise above self-love. Even when he is in a relationship with another person, George will evaluate the relationship and the other person only in terms of whether it is making George happy. When George does hook up, he will invariably wind up not with a life partner whom he will know and who will know him but with an image of himself: Narcissus will find his Echo.

Mammas and Poppas

If Eve helps Adam to know himself and Adam helps Eve to know herself, then the addition of children amplifies the self-knowledge. In becoming mothers and fathers, we truly become ourselves and come to know ourselves. Recall my conversation with engaged couples recounted in chapter 8: Our identity as human beings is intrinsically connected with our identity as men and women; and the definition of a man is a human with male reproductive organs, and the definition of a woman is a person with female reproductive organs. Those organs were designed for procreation, so to be fully human — to operate as a human was designed — is to be a father or a mother.

Procreation, therefore, helps us to know ourselves, but rearing children *really* brings us to the point of self-knowledge. Every child born to a couple is also a lifetime commitment of love, but this time we don't get to choose. Children are given to us by divine providence, and in relationship with those children, our own identities are affirmed even more profoundly. We are approved of and recognized by our children as mothers and fathers, and in turn we recognize and approve of them — affirming and confirming their identities as dignified, worthy, lovable human beings.

The Creatively Subversive Solution

This is why I conclude my conversation with engaged couples by saying, "I know! Why don't the two of you do something really wild, crazy, and subversive!"

They look at me with sudden bewilderment. This is a Catholic priest, right? He's telling us to go crazy and be subversive.

"What I'm suggesting is this," I continue. "In this society and culture, where there is a total sexual free-for-all, why not be really countercultural and subversive: get married, stay married, have lots of children, and practice your Catholic Faith."

I then explain how our parish is helping couples do this. We encourage them to live and work locally and to join the parish. We ask them to put their kids in our parish school. We offer financial assistance to young families if they need it. If their kids are enrolled in our school, they pay tuition for only two children. The rest attend free. If they homeschool, we help them with curriculum and networking in the homeschool community.

The creatively subversive solution is not to weep and wail and blame the "sinners" for their eroticism. The reasons the culture has gone into expressive individualism, sentimentalism, and eroticism are complex and reach back two hundred years and more. Furthermore, one of the reasons society has gone in the direction it has is the failure of Christians to understand the goodness of faithful marriage and to explain and support it for its intrinsic good — not just as a conventional, respectable, "good Christian" thing to do.

The remedy, therefore, is to support marriage and family life creatively, positively, and compassionately. With the affluence we enjoy, authentic marriage and family life should be easier than ever before. It seems, however, that it is more difficult than ever before. The complications of modern life, the underlying atheistic philosophies we have discussed, and the weakness of the Church in the face of these obstacles have made the witness of authentic marriage and family life a huge challenge. However, where the darkness is deepest, the light is the brightest. Where we do have strong families, strong parishes, and a joyful witness, the attraction is so great that many others wish to join. We must be ready to welcome them.

I Was Chaste, but She Caught Me

In the face of a sexually dissolute society, the Catholic Faith has always supported an even more creatively subversive alternative: celibacy. Catholic priests and religious offer their sexuality completely. In a vow of celibacy, they promise not only to remain single but to sleep alone and never enjoy sexual intimacy.

If marriage and family life seem to the libertines to be an absurd social restriction, the idea of celibacy is even more of an outrage. It must be admitted that some of the defenses of celibacy have been motivated by a misplaced negativity toward the physical realm. In other words, "Sex is dirty and sinful and truly holy people never do anything dirty and sinful." This is a heresy that flies in the face of God's very first commandment to the human race: "Be fertile and multiply" (Gen. 1:28). If sex is dirty and sinful, God wouldn't have commanded us to do it.

Although sexuality is the great gift to humanity, however, it is also the great curse. Satan loves to distort and destroy human sexuality because he knows that it is the foundation of our identities and the process and principle of love. He hates us. He hates our identity, and he therefore hates marriage, families, and true love.

Celibacy is the priest's and religious's way of defeating Satan's distortions completely. The vow of celibacy does not negate sex and married love. Paradoxically, it affirms that sexual and married love have a higher purpose and meaning. The person who takes a vow of celibacy affirms that total self-giving is possible. The priest, monk, or nun says to the married person, "This total self-giving to God is what your married love is all about. This is the higher purpose and meaning of your love: that it will move beyond mere sexual union to a mystical union with Christ, the Bridegroom."

In return, in the mystery of the Church, the married couple say to the priest, monk, or nun, "And do you see us? This is what the nuptial union means. Our lifelong, complementary union, our union of self-knowing and self-giving is what your love of God is like. As husband and wife are one flesh, so your union with Christ, the Bridegroom, is mystical and complete. As we know and are known in marriage, you know and are known in your union with Him."

Finally, this is why the husband and wife are chaste within marriage. Chastity is different from celibacy. Celibacy is a vow that excludes sexual activity completely. Chastity excludes all sexual activity outside of marriage. Chastity is for all Christians. Celibacy is for those with a particular vow to celibacy. For those who are unmarried, celibacy is the expression of their chastity. For those who are married, chastity is expressed by complete faithfulness to the marriage vow. Adultery breaks marital chastity. Fornication breaks the unmarried person's chastity.

In a highly sexualized world, chastity is subversive indeed. Furthermore, chastity pulls the rug out from under Freudianism. Freud, like Rousseau before him, argued that society's restraints on sexual activity caused repression and sickness. Furthermore, it was religion that caused the most restrictions on the freedoms of human sexual instinct. One can see why Freud and Rousseau thought this. They were in a society in which the Christian religion was the default setting and the Christian code of sexual morality was the accepted standard of law and respectability. In their day, Christian society did impose a standard of sexual morality.

Beheading Hydra

Ending the Consultation with Dr. Freud

We are no longer in that situation; we can thank God that we are no longer in a society that is so legalistic. The sexual revolution has allowed people not only to make bad choices but also to make good choices. This means that one now lives by the Christian code of sexual morality by choice, not merely from religious and social pressure.

This is truly subversive because it says to Dr. Freud:

You tell me that my sexual urges are irresistible — that I am a brute beast ruled by my animalistic desires to rut according to my basic urges. How dare you! I'm telling you that I am better than that. I am not a brute beast, and I am not dominated by animalistic instincts beyond my control. I am a human being, and I can make choices about my body.

You say religion oppresses me and restricts my sexual happiness. Religion may have been restrictive in your day, but it's not anymore. Now everybody may do as he likes and society approves just as you would have wished. Therefore, your argument about religion being cruelly restrictive doesn't apply.

Therefore, as an act of my free will — and without any coercion by anyone or by any code or creed — I am choosing to be chaste.

I'm telling you, Dr. Fraud, that I am freely choosing the path of self-discipline, self-control, and the higher calling of chastity. I am choosing this way because it is the path of human dignity. You can go tell your clever French friend Rousseau that I am also not a slave to my sweet romantic feelings. You can tell your crazy pal Nietzsche that my morality is not determined by my being a slave to a religious hierarchy. I have chosen this path myself, and, while you're at it, you can go tell your friend Charles Darwin that I am more than the result of random biological destiny. I am choosing this way because it is the path of ultimate human happiness. I am choosing this way in order to know myself, to know another person, and, ultimately, to know God.

The fact that my choice goes contrary to my most basic instincts is proof that it is a free and willing choice. Anybody can follow his libido. I'm choosing liberty.

Finally, Sigmund, my chastity also corrects your pathetic, sophomoric atheism because, in choosing freely to control my so-called brute instincts, I am proving that they do not control me. I am proving that I have free will, and if I have free will—a desire and a power that is higher than brutal biology—it was given to me by Someone who is even greater than me and greater than all the biological forces. And the only One who could be greater is the One who created them, and I'm sorry, truly sorry, that you never got to know Him.

18

No Respect

You may say, "Fr. Longenecker, you promised a 'radical plan for Christians in an atheistic age.' You have simply given us the same old story." Perhaps. But I never said it was new. I said it was radical. I have challenged you to get back to the basics — to the root and foundation of it all.

One of the problems with Christianity is that it has become respectable instead of radical. The old respectability used to be large, suburban families trooping off to a building that looked like a church on Sunday. The new respectability is small, suburban families trooping off to a building that looks like a supermarket. The old-fashioned respectables attended First Presbyterian, First Baptist, St John's Episcopal, Trinity Lutheran, St. Paul the Apostle, or United Methodist. The new respectables worship at Newspring, Resolute, Upsurge, GraceFull, Grapevine, Relevance, ReBound, or Skyfall.

But respectable doesn't work anymore — neither the old respectable or the new respectable. What is needed is the radicalism I have described. This is the old, old story, lived out in a new way.

In every age, the radical, authentic Christian message is strange and terrible, beautiful and new. If we could only see it, we would share the passion and thrill of St. Augustine centuries ago. He wrote at a time when the Roman Empire was sinking into the swamp of decadence and lawlessness and crumbling into chaos. St. Augustine caught the vision and saw how creative and subversive this beautiful faith really is. So he wrote in his *Confessions*:

> Late have I loved you, O Beauty ever ancient, ever new, late have I loved you! You were within me, but I was outside, and it was there that I searched for you. In my unloveliness I plunged into the lovely things which you created. You were with me, but I was not with you. Created things kept me from you; yet if they had not been in you, they would have not been at all. You called, you shouted, and you broke through my deafness. You flashed, you shone, and you dispelled my blindness. You breathed your fragrance on me; I drew in breath, and now I pant for you. I have tasted you, now I hunger and thirst for more. You touched me, and I burned for your peace. (10, 27, 38)

This is the radical vision each Christian must yearn for in the present dark days. The radical solution is not political. It is not accomplished through manifestos, gimmicks, and religious tricks. The radical solution does not come from religious hierarchs and spiritual gurus. The radical answer is not one of mere emotional experience and does not come from the pressure of preachers.

The radical solution comes as individuals are touched with the fire of the Holy Spirit and called by that beauty that is ever ancient and ever new. It comes as they bind themselves to the Church, which gives them stability and roots their small lives into the greater community we call the Mystical Body of Christ. However, as Ralph Martin has shown in *A Church in Crisis*, the

Church as she now stands is herself in turmoil and disintegration. We should be prepared to see the old ways of "doing church" crumble. During the pandemic of 2020, churches were closed and Mass obligations were suspended. Will all those churchgoers return? Will church life ever be the same?

It is time to build again from the ground up. If we live this radical example at the local level — in our families, our schools, our parishes, our wider communities — then we will be living out the creatively subversive solution. Rod Dreher, in both *The Benedict Option* and *Live Not by Lies*, has read the signs of the times and has called for local units of faith and family to be the depositories of Christian culture and the seedbed for renewal.

We are conditioned to expect instant success, but this will not happen. We will not see immediate results. Instead, we will probably see some serious setbacks — even persecution. God plays a long game. In the sixth century, St. Benedict went out to form simple communities rooted in work, prayer, and reading. Eventually, they bore fruit and provided the foundation for one thousand years of Christian culture. But St. Benedict could never have seen that. He died before it all came to pass.

So it is for Christians in our age. We will, no doubt, continue to see our own culture slide into the swamp of relativism and the quicksand of individualistic desire. I fully expect a continued upsurge of violence in our culture, and perhaps the emergence of a modern, high-tech totalitarian state will manifest itself, offering security and safety for citizens while quietly destroying their freedoms.

Whatever the future holds, the creatively subversive solution is the answer. With it, we will build peace and our own security; we will build a future for our Faith, our families, and a new Christendom. It can be done if we each, like St. Benedict and like so many other examples down through history, pick up the torch and do what we can where we are, with what we have, "running in the way of God's commandments, our hearts overflowing with an inexpressible delight of love."[58]

---

[58] Rule of St. Benedict, prologue, 49.

Bibliography

Aeschliman, Michael D. *The Restitution of Man, C. S. Lewis and the Case against Scientism*. Grand Rapids, MI: William B. Eerdmans, 1998.

Allen, John L., Jr. *The Future Church: How Ten Trends Are Revolutionizing the Catholic Church*. New York: Doubleday, 2009.

Augustine of Hippo. *The City of God*. New York: Image Books, 1954.

Barzun, Jacques. *From Dawn to Decadence: 500 Years of Western Cultural Life*. New York: Harper Collins, 2000.

Belloc, Hilaire. *Survivals and New Arrivals*. Rockford, IL: Tan Books, 1992.

Berlin, Isaiah. *The Crooked Timber of Humanity*. Princeton: Princeton University Press, 2013.

Brumfield, Joshua. *The Benedict Proposal*. Eugene, OR: Pickwick Publications, 2020.

DeWohl, Louis, *The Citadel of God*. San Francisco: Ignatius Press, 1959.

Douthat, Ross. *Bad Religion: How We Became a Nation of Heretics* New York: Free Press, 2012.

————. *To Change the Church*. New York: Simon and Schuster, 2018.

————. *The Decadent Society: How We Became Victims of Our Own Success*. New York: Avid Reader Press, 2020.

Dostoevsky, Fyodor. *The Brothers Karamazov*. New York: Random House, 1950.

Dreher, Rod, *The Benedict Option: A Strategy for Christians in a Post-Christian Nation*. New York: Sentinel, 2018.

———. *Live Not by Lies*. New York: Sentinel, 2020.

Eliot, T. S., *The Complete Poems and Plays*. New York: Harcourt, Brace and World, 1971.

Esolen, Anthony. *Out of the Ashes: Rebuilding American Culture*. Washington, DC: Regnery, 2017.

Farmer, David Hugh. *Benedict's Disciples*. Herefordshire, UK: Gracewing, 1995.

Ferrara, Christopher, and Thomas E. Woods, Jr. *The Great Façade: The Regime of Novelty in the Catholic Church from Vatican II to the Francis Revolution*. Brooklyn, NY: Angelico Press, 2015.

Freud, Sigmund. *Civilization and Its Discontents*. New York: Penguin, 2002.

Girard, René. *The Scapegoat*. Translated by Yvonne Freccero. Baltimore: John Hopkins University Press, 1986.

Gregg, Samuel. *Reason, Faith, and the Struggle for Western Civilization*. Washington, DC: Regnery Gateway, 2019.

Holland, Tom. *Dominion: How the Christian Revolution Remade the World*. New York: Basic Books, 2019.

John Paul II, *Fides et Ratio*. Boston: Pauline Books and Media, 1988.

Jones, E. Michael. *Degenerate Moderns: Modernity as Rationalized Sexual Misbehavior*. San Francisco: Ignatius Press, 1993.

Lewis, C. S. *The Abolition of Man*. New York: MacMillan, 1955.

———. *The Four Loves*. San Francisco: HarperOne, 2017.

———. *God in the Dock: Essays on Theology and Ethics*. Edited by Walter Hooper. Grand Rapids, MI: William B. Eerdmans, 1970.

———. *Perelandra*. New York: Scribner, 1972.

———. *The Silver Chair*. New York: MacMillan, 1971.

Martin, Ralph. *A Church in Crisis, Pathways Forward*. Steubenville, OH: Emmaus, 2020.

McInerny, Ralph. *Art and Prudence: Studies in the Thought of Jacques Maritain*. Notre Dame, IN: Notre Dame University Press, 1988.

Bibliography

Minoni, Anthony, Jr., ed. *The Popes against Modern Errors: Sixteen Papal Documents*. Charlotte, NC: Tan Books, 1999.

Moczar, Diane. *The Church under Attack*. Manchester, NH: Sophia Institute Press, 2013.

Murray, Douglas. *The Madness of Crowds: Gender, Race, and Identity*. London: Bloomsbury, 2020.

Newman, John Henry. *Essay on the Development of Doctrine*. Kerry, Ireland: Crossreach, 2018.

Nicholi, Armand, Jr. *The Question of God: C.S.Lewis and Sigmund Freud Debate God, Love, Sex, and the Meaning of Life*. New York: Free Press, 2002.

Nietzsche, Friedrich. *Beyond Good and Evil*. New York: SDE Classics, 2019.

———. *On the Genealogy of Morality*. 3rd ed. Edited by Keith Ansell-Pearson. Cambridge, UK: Cambridge University Press, 2017.

Pieper, Josef. *The Four Cardinal Virtues*. Notre Dame, IN: Notre Dame University Press, 1966.

Ratzinger, Joseph. *On the Way to Jesus Christ*. San Francisco: Ignatius Press, 2004.

Reno, R.R. *The Return of the Strong Gods: Nationalism, Populism, and the Future of the West*. Washington, DC: Regnery Gateway, 2019.

Rutler, George W. *Beyond Modernity*. San Francisco: Ignatius Press, 1987.

———. *A Crisis in Culture: How Secularism is Becoming a Religion*. Irondale, AL: EWTN Publishing, 2020.

Sarah, Cardinal Robert. *The Day Is Now Far Spent*. San Francisco: Ignatius Press, 2019.

———. *God or Nothing*. San Francisco: Ignatius Press, 2015.

Senior, John. *The Restoration of Christian Culture*. Norfolk, VA: IHS Press, 2008.

Scheler, Max. *Ressentiment*. Milwaukee: Marquette University Press, 2013.

Sheen, Fulton J. *Communism and the Conscience of the West*. Pekin, IN: Refuge of Sinners Publishing, 1948.

———. *Life of Christ*. New York: McGraw-Hill, 1958.

Storey, Benjamin, and Jenna Silber Storey. *Why We Are Restless: On the Modern Quest for Contentment*. Princeton: Princeton University Press, 2021.

Stark, Rodney. *Cities of God: The Real Story of How Christianity Became an Urban Movement and Conquered Rome*. New York: HarperOne, 2009.

Stuart, Joseph. *Rethinking the Enlightenment: Faith in the Age of Reason*. Manchester, NH: Sophia Institute Press, 2020.

Trueman, Carl R. *The Rise and Triumph of the Modern Self: Cultural Amnesia, Expressive Individualism, and the Road to Sexual Revolution*. Wheaton, IL: Crossway, 2020.

Taylor, Charles. *A Secular Age*. Cambridge, MA: Belknap Press, 2007.

Tyson, Jon, and Heather Grizzle. *A Creative Minority: Influencing Culture through Redemptive Participation*. Self-published, 2016.

Wiedenkopf, Steve. *Timeless: A History of the Catholic Church*. Huntington, IN: Our Sunday Visitor, 2018.

Weigel, George. *Evangelical Catholicism: Deep Reform in the 21st-Century Church*. New York: Basic Books, 2013.

———. *The Irony of Modern Catholic History: How the Church Rediscovered Itself and Challenged the Modern World to Reform*. New York: Basic Books, 2019.

About the Author

Fr. Dwight Longenecker was brought up in an Evangelical home in Pennsylvania and studied English and speech at Bob Jones University before being trained for ministry in the Church of England at Oxford. He served for fifteen years as an Anglican priest before he and his family were received into the Catholic Church.

In 2006, Fr. Longenecker returned to the United States to be ordained a Catholic priest under the pastoral provision for married former Protestant ministers. He now serves as the pastor of Our Lady of the Rosary parish in Greenville, South Carolina. He is married to Alison, and they have four grown children.

Fr. Longenecker is the author of more than twenty books on Catholic Faith and culture. His blog, *Standing on My Head*, is one of the most widely read Catholic blogs. Fr. Longenecker also contributes to a wide range of magazines, journals, websites, and podcasts. You can follow his writings, listen to his podcasts, join his online courses, browse his books, and be in touch at DwightLongenecker.com.

Sophia Institute

Sophia Institute is a nonprofit institution that seeks to nurture the spiritual, moral, and cultural life of souls and to spread the gospel of Christ in conformity with the authentic teachings of the Roman Catholic Church.

Sophia Institute Press fulfills this mission by offering translations, reprints, and new publications that afford readers a rich source of the enduring wisdom of mankind.

Sophia Institute also operates the popular online resource CatholicExchange.com. *Catholic Exchange* provides world news from a Catholic perspective as well as daily devotionals and articles that will help readers to grow in holiness and live a life consistent with the teachings of the Church.

In 2013, Sophia Institute launched Sophia Institute for Teachers to renew and rebuild Catholic culture through service to Catholic education. With the goal of nurturing the spiritual, moral, and cultural life of souls, and an abiding respect for the role and work of teachers, we strive to provide materials and programs that are at once enlightening to the mind and ennobling to the heart; faithful and complete, as well as useful and practical.

Sophia Institute gratefully recognizes the Solidarity Association for preserving and encouraging the growth of our apostolate over the course of many years. Without their generous and timely support, this book would not be in your hands.

www.SophiaInstitute.com
www.CatholicExchange.com
www.SophiaInstituteforTeachers.org

Sophia Institute Press® is a registered trademark of Sophia Institute.
Sophia Institute is a tax-exempt institution as defined by the
Internal Revenue Code, Section 501(c)(3). Tax ID 22-2548708.